EXPEN
WARRIORS

The Stackpole Military History Series

THE AMERICAN CIVIL WAR

Cavalry Raids of the Civil War
Ghost, Thunderbolt, and Wizard
Pickett's Charge
Witness to Gettysburg

WORLD WAR I

Doughboy War

WORLD WAR II

Armor Battles of the Waffen-SS,
  1943–45
Armoured Guardsmen
Army of the West
Australian Commandos
The B-24 in China
Backwater War
The Battle of Sicily
Beyond the Beachhead
The Brandenburger Commandos
The Brigade
Bringing the Thunder
Coast Watching in
  World War II
Colossal Cracks
A Dangerous Assignment
D-Day Deception
D-Day to Berlin
Destination Normandy
Dive Bomber!
A Drop Too Many
Eagles of the Third Reich
Eastern Front Combat
Exit Rommel
Fist from the Sky
Flying American Combat
  Aircraft of World War II
Forging the Thunderbolt
Fortress France
The German Defeat in the East,
  1944–45
German Order of Battle, Vol. 1
German Order of Battle, Vol. 2
German Order of Battle, Vol. 3
The Germans in Normandy

Germany's Panzer Arm in
  World War II
GI Ingenuity
Goodwood
The Great Ships
Grenadiers
Hitler's Nemesis
Infantry Aces
Iron Arm
Iron Knights
Kampfgruppe Peiper at the
  Battle of the Bulge
Kursk
Luftwaffe Aces
Massacre at Tobruk
Mechanized Juggernaut or
  Military Anachronism?
Messerschmitts over Sicily
Michael Wittmann, Vol. 1
Michael Wittmann, Vol. 2
Mountain Warriors
The Nazi Rocketeers
On the Canal
Operation Mercury
Packs On!
Panzer Aces
Panzer Aces II
Panzer Commanders of the
  Western Front
The Panzer Legions
Panzers in Normandy
Panzers in Winter
The Path to Blitzkrieg
Penalty Strike
Red Star under the Baltic
Retreat to the Reich
Rommel's Desert Commanders
Rommel's Desert War
Rommel's Lieutenants
The Savage Sky
A Soldier in the Cockpit
Soviet Blitzkrieg
Stalin's Keys to Victory
Surviving Bataan and Beyond
T-34 in Action
Tank Tactics

Tigers in the Mud
Triumphant Fox
The 12th SS, Vol. 1
The 12th SS, Vol. 2
The War against Rommel's
  Supply Lines
War in the Aegean
Wolfpack Warriors

THE COLD WAR / VIETNAM

Cyclops in the Jungle
Expendable Warriors
Flying American Combat
  Aircraft: The Cold War
Here There Are Tigers
Land with No Sun
Phantom Reflections
Street without Joy
Through the Valley

WARS OF THE MIDDLE EAST

Never-Ending Conflict

GENERAL MILITARY HISTORY

Carriers in Combat
Desert Battles
Guerrilla Warfare

EXPENDABLE WARRIORS

The Battle of Khe Sanh
and the Vietnam War

Bruce B. G. Clarke

STACKPOLE
BOOKS

Published in paperback in 2009 by
STACKPOLE BOOKS
5067 Ritter Road
Mechanicsburg, PA 17055
www.stackpolebooks.com

EXPENDABLE WARRIORS: THE BATTLE OF KHE SANH AND THE VIETNAM
WAR, by Bruce B. G. Clarke, was originally published in hard cover by Praeger
Security International, an imprint of Greenwood Publishing Group, Inc., Westport,
CT. Copyright © 2007 by Bruce Clarke Consultants, Inc. Paperback edition by
arrangement with Greenwood Publishing Group, Inc. All rights reserved.

Cover design by Tracy Patterson

Printed in the United States of America

10 9 8 7 6 5 4 3 2 1

ISBN 978-0-8117-3537-7 (Stackpole paperback)

The Library of Congress has cataloged the hardcover edition as follows:

Clarke, Bruce B. G., 1943–
    Expendable warriors : the Battle of Khe Sanh and the Vietnam War / Bruce B.
G. Clark ; foreword by John W. Vessey.
        p. cm.
    Includes bibliographical references and index.
    ISBN-13: 978-0-275-99480-8 (alk. paper)
    ISBN-10: 0-275-99480-5 (alk. paper)
    1. Khe Sanh, Battle of, Vietnam, 1968. I. Title.
DS557.8.K5C56 2007
959.704'342—dc22   2006038655

Contents

Foreword

Colonel Bruce Clarke is known for his strategic acumen and tactical ability. *Expendable Warriors: The Battle of Khe Sanh and the Vietnam War* demonstrates this acumen and the roots of his tactical ability. Using a masterful blend of oral history and research, he interweaves first-hand recollections of fellow Khe Sanh veterans with rigorously researched material and sound tactical and strategic analysis.

Colonel Clarke had a unique perspective on the battles that raged on the Khe Sanh plateau in early 1968. He had been there since August of 1967. As a young captain and district advisor he led the valiant defense of the District Headquarters against an enemy force of possibly regimental size. Actual participants—the advisory team medic, Jim Perry and Corpsman John Roberts describe this defense. The aviators of the 282nd Helicopter Company tell their story of being ambushed and having several of their own men become possible prisoners of war (POWs).

The fight around the village, in my opinion, ranks among the most resounding victories at Khe Sanh, and has never been adequately or correctly reported in extant histories. Though statistically a small action, the completeness of the victory against overwhelming odds is in itself enough to merit notice. However, at the strategic level, it illustrates General C. Westmoreland's (commander of U.S. forces in Vietnam) goal of enticing the North Vietnamese into a fight around Khe Sanh. In this effort, the men with Colonel Clarke were expendable. To evacuate them would have tipped Westmoreland's hand and compromised his intelligence sources. *Expendable Warriors* correctly analyzes the strategic issues imbedded in Westmoreland's decision. Colonel Clarke highlights that at the operational level this may have been a reasonable approach, but because the battles around Khe Sanh lasted 77 days and the "agony of Khe Sanh" played in the press for that period this series of battles was, as pointed out, the culminating point of the Vietnam War. It is this ability to present and analyze at multiple levels that make this work must reading for anyone who wants to understand the totality that is war.

As a participant in the siege of the Khe Sanh Combat Base, Colonel Clarke makes this Dien Bien Phu like battle come to life in the trenches and bunkers that were that part of the battle. As a participant in the planning for the relief operation, he observes and reports a previously unknown discussion that shows the direct impact of political decisions on combat operations.

Colonel Bruce Clarke's telling the "Untold Story of Khe Sanh" is an important addition to the entire history of the Vietnamese War—an addition to the history that needs to be read by everyone.

Colonel Clarke's analyses of the events around Khe Sanh are must reading for future combat leaders. He points out not only the mistakes that were made at the tactical and strategic level, but also suggests what should have been done. This analysis sets this effort above every study of Vietnam that I have seen.

In telling this story Colonel Clarke and the other participants make the horrors and sacrifices of war come to life. The reader will understand the fate of the Bru Montagnard tribe and why some survivors of Khe Sanh several times a year return with funds and other help for these neglected people who were such staunch allies.

Expendable Warriors should be read by anyone who is interested in understanding the root causes of the way that the Vietnam War ended.

I support, in the final analysis, Colonel Clarke's admonition that "we need to learn from our mistakes and ensure that we don't repeat them. We owe it to the next generation of brave soldiers, sailors, airmen, and marines that they will not have to endure similar tests of their courage and determination."

John W. Vessey
General, U.S. Army (retired)

Preface

If you take a flat map and move wooden blocks on it, they behave as they should. The science of war is moving live men like blocks. Getting wooden squares into position at the right time. But it takes time to mold men into blocks. Flat maps turn into rivers and gullies, and you can't pick them up in your hand to move them.

It's all so clear on the map: Blocks curling around other blocks and crunching them up ... But men get tired and orders are slow. You move too slowly and take too long. It's not like it was on the map. And soldiers die ...

—Stephen Vincent Benet, *John Brown's Body*, 1928

In the foreword to Dave Stockwell's book *Tanks in the Wire,* about the fall of the Lang Vei Special Forces Camp, I wrote:

Tanks in the Wire! is about a battle in Vietnam, which was in itself and in the overall scheme of things, probably relatively insignificant. However, what it tells us about success and failure in combat provides lessons which, as a nation, we should learn and learn well.

Army Chief of Staff General Douglas MacArthur, known for saying, "There is no substitute for victory," wrote in 1935:

The military student does not seek to learn from history the minutia and technique. In every age these are decisively influenced by the characteristics of weapons currently available and by the means at hand for maneuvering, supplying and controlling combat forces. But research does bring to light those *fundamental principles,* and their *combinations* and *applications,* which, in the past, have been productive of success. These principles know no limitations of time. Consequently, the Army extends its analytical interest to the dust-buried accounts of wars long past as well as to those still reeking with the scent of battle.

This narrative provides those lessons by looking at thoughts and observations of the author and other participants as they relate to the battles around the Khe Sanh Combat Base in 1968. The January to April 1968 siege of the Marine Corps Combat Base in the Northwestern corner of South Vietnam was the turning point in the political and military outcome of the Vietnam War. The North Vietnamese lost the battle for the Combat Base, even though they suffered huge losses in "winning" the battles of Khe Sanh village and Lang Vei. In this case, winning means gaining physical control of the facilities in those two locations. But did the North Vietnamese lose? They argue that because the Combat Base was evacuated following the relief of the siege they had won. I am not sure that terrain occupation is winning, but I am sure that their ability to keep the "agony of Khe Sanh" on the front pages of the daily papers and on everyone's TV screens for more than 2 months accomplished their psychological goal. As Clausewitz points out, tactical victories should not be ends, but means to ends. The North Vietnamese understood this. Did we? The reader will come to know the agony, the heroism, and the impact of this battle on history through the contributions of several of the participants in the different parts of the battle.

This book has taken a long time to be written partially because the author put the events behind him and got on with the job of being a soldier. For some of the other participants, recalling events and emotions that occurred 38 years ago was difficult. They had long ago buried the pain deep in the recesses of their minds, where it was locked and inaccessible to reflection until now. The writing of this story has been a trail of tears for some, a cleansing for others.

The experience was like a mural done on a large piece of glass. A greater being dropped the pane of glass breaking it into pieces. Each of the participants left Khe Sanh with different pieces of the broken picture and like the ten blind, wise men, each memory was partially right, and each partially wrong. Putting the mural of that experience back together is the goal of this book. Perhaps now, each participant, having a small piece of the picture, can add it to the greater work and we shall know the truth about what happened at Khe Sanh.

It has taken me 35 years to return to the uneasiness of our story. Resurrecting the memory of lost comrades, lost wars, and lost opportunities can be onerous business and easily put aside. But the time has come to try and put the pieces back together again. Perhaps our pain and experience will stand as an ensign to future warriors. We recount our sorrows that they will learn from these experiences and will find themselves better prepared to deal with the horrors and passions of war. The participants of this battle want you to know how they feel about war. It's important to learn from the mistakes that were made so that they will not be repeated. The men whose stories are on these pages do this by sharing with you a few of the memorable experiences at Khe Sanh and attempt to put them into historical perspective. Men who have risked all for their country will understand the purpose of this book—we challenge policymakers to also learn the effects of political decisions on tactical realities.

Acknowledgments

This volume would not have been possible without the efforts of the participants of that battle. Thanks are in order to James Perry, John Roberts, Major (MAJ) Tinh-A-Nhi and a number of others who have shared their thoughts, memories, and insight. The principal participants, whose experiences are quoted in this work, came to Khe Sanh from different backgrounds and went on to completely different and productive lives. Khe Sanh had a lasting impact on their lives—good and bad—but each was able to overcome the negative aspects and to be a productive member of society. Jim Perry, John Roberts, and Bruce Clarke each had long military careers. Jim Perry retired and passed away early in 2006. We regret that he did not see his valor and humor published before his passing. John Roberts runs his own investment advisory company in Canyon, Texas. Bruce Clarke is a retired colonel after 30 years on active duty and is a defense consultant and author of articles of strategic and political importance.

In addition to the participants noted above the contributions of other warriors from Khe Sanh are appreciated. I must thank Jim Whitenack, Harlan E. "Rip" Van Winkle, Grenville Sutcliffe, Dan Kelley, Ward Britt, Bob Donoghue, Jaime Taronji, and Delores Amos-Bayer, the widow of George Amos. Tom Pullen, Paul Callaway, Richard Brittingham, and the rest of the Black Cats are also due thanks, for their contributions are critical to making this story complete. Brian Johnson is to be thanked for his efforts at turning very rough drawings into finalized maps. Donna Elliott's contribution of the information on her brother Jerry and her search for closure on his disappearance is greatly appreciated. Her story is gripping. From the historical vignettes recounted in this effort, one cannot help but appreciate the contributions of all of the Combined Action Company (CAC) OSCAR Marines, the U.S. Army Special Forces at Forward Operating Base-3 (FOB-3) and Lang Vei, MAJ Tinh-A-Nhi, the Vietnamese soldiers of 915th Regional Force Company, the 282nd Air Mobile Light Company, and most importantly the Bru Montagnards of the area—soldiers and noncombatants. They were expendable, but didn't know it and their gallantry and devotion saw them through some very trying times that are recounted in the following pages. A special gratitude is due for the families of dead soldiers that were left behind on the battlefield. Their families, besides receiving some monetary compensation from the Vietnamese Government, never got any recognition for their valiant efforts. Finally I would like to thank Lt. Colonel (LTC) (ret) Peter Kindsvater for his detailed review and especially thank Shelia Cosper for her insightful editing and willingness to learn the intricacies and challenges of combat.

Bruce B. G. Clarke
Colonel, U.S. Army (retired)

Abbreviations

AID	Agency for International Development
AML	Air Mobile Light
ARVN	Army Republic of Vietnam
ASAP	As Soon As Possible
CA	Combat Assault
CAC	Combined Action Company
CAP	Combined Action Platoon
CIA	Central Intelligence Agency
CIDG	Civilian Irregular Defense Force—a force run by Vietnamese Special Forces
CINCPAC	Commander in Chief Pacific
COFRAM	Controlled Fragmentation Munitions
COL	Colonel
COMUSMACV	Commander, United States Military Command Vietnam
CPL	Corporal
CPT	Captain (Army)
CW2	Chief Warrant Officer Two
DIA	Defense Intelligence Agency
DMZ	Demilitarized Zone
DPMO	Defense Prisoner of War/Missing Personnel Office
EGT	Exhaust Gas Temperature
FAC	Forward Air Controller
FMF	Fleet Marine Force

FOB	Forward Operating Base
GVN	Government of Vietnam
HQ	Headquarters
JCS	Joint Chiefs of Staff
JPAC	Joint Personnel Accounting Command
JTAD	Joint Technical Advisory Detachment
JTF-FA	Joint Task Force—Full Accounting Team
KIA	Killed in Action
KSCB	Khe Sanh Combat Base
LAPES	Low Altitude Parachute Extraction System
LAW	Light Anti-Tank Weapon
LBJ	Lyndon Baines Johnson
LCPL or L/CPL	Lance Corporal
LRRP	Long Range Reconnaissance Patrol
LT	Lieutenant
LTC	Lieutenant Colonel
LTG	Lieutenant General
LZ	Landing Zone
MACV	Military Assistance Command Vietnam
MACV-SOG	Military Assistance Command Vietnam, Studies and Observation Group
MD	Doctor of Medicine
MEDCCAP	Medical-Civil Action Program
MG	Machine Gun
MIA	Missing in Action
MR	Machine Records
NCO	Non-Commissioned Officer
NGO	Non-Governmental Organization
NOD	Night Observation Device
NVA	North Vietnamese Army
OB/GYN	Obstetrician/Gynecologist
OSS	Office of Strategic Studies
PF	Popular Force
PFC	Private First Class
POL	Petroleum, Oil and Lubricants
POW	Prisoner of War
PSP	Pierced Steel Planking
RF	Regional Force
RPG	Rocket-Propelled Grenade
RPM	Revolutions Per Minute
SFC	Sergeant First Class
SGT	Sergeant
SIGINT	Signals Intelligence

SOG	Study and Observation Group—also called Special Operations Group by some
SP/4 also SP4	Specialist Fourth Class—the Army equivalent of a Marine Corporal
SP/5 also SP5 and Spec 5	Specialist Fifth Class, next grade above SP/4. For pay purposes equivalent to a SGT
SSGT	Staff Sergeant
TB	Tuberculosis
TDY	Temporary Duty
III MAF	Third Marine Amphibious Force
US	United States
USAF	United States Air Force
USAID	United States Agency for International Development
USMC	United States Marine Corps
VC	Viet Cong
VIP	Very Important Person
VT	Variable Time
WO	Warrant Officer
WW II	World War II

Chapter 1

District Headquarters
Village of Khe Sanh
January 22, 1968, early in the morning

The Communists were about to capture their first political headquarters. The District Headquarters in the village of Khe Sanh had become a throwaway in General (GEN) Westmoreland's efforts to shore up his own credibility after having argued that we "could see the light at the end of the tunnel." The political mood in the United States was swinging against the war and a victory was needed to ensure public support and President Lyndon Johnson's political future.

William Childs Westmoreland graduated from the United States Military Academy in 1936. He had a distinguished career leading up to his assignment as the commander of Military Assistance Command, Vietnam, and all U.S. forces in Vietnam. His notable assignments include chief of staff of the 9th Infantry Division in the closing operations of World War II in Germany, command of the 504th Parachute Infantry, 82nd Airborne Division, later becoming the division chief of staff. He commanded the 187th Airborne Regimental Combat Team in operations in Korea, 1952–1953. After command of the 101st Airborne Division and Fort Campbell, he became the superintendent of the United States Military Academy, 1960–1963. He went from there to command the Strategic Army Corps and XVIII Airborne Corps and then was successively deputy commander and acting commander of United States Military Assistance Command, Vietnam. His final position on active duty was as chief of staff of the United States Army where he supervised the Army's disengagement from Vietnam, the transition from the draft to an all-volunteer footing, and the employment of troops in a period of active civil disturbance.

Westmoreland knew that the North Vietnamese Army (NVA) was moving toward the Marine Combat Base at Khe Sanh, in the northwestern corner of South Vietnam. He wanted to entice the North Vietnamese into a firepower-intensive battle, for he thought that it could be decisive in his attrition strategy for changing public opinion back home and winning the war. Westmoreland's goal was not to seize territory but to kill on such a scale that the NVA would either lose its will or be unable to replace its losses. But Westmoreland underestimated the forces of resistance.

The initial NVA assault would be against the small District Headquarters in the village of Khe Sanh—a small but strategic outpost 5 miles from the Combat Base. Like Churchill, who sacrificed Coventry for Ultra, Westmoreland was willing to sacrifice the District Headquarters for public sentiment and the sake of secrecy. Churchill, knowing from the code intercept program called Ultra that Coventry was to be bombed, did not alert the city for fear of compromising the source of the information. Westmoreland seems to have acted the same way as Churchill over notifying the forces in the village headquarters.

The mixed force of Army advisors, Marines, Vietnamese, and tribal warriors in the village were the bait to get the NVA to move toward the Combat Base. To that end the warriors in this small compound had been left uninformed of the approaching North Vietnamese enemy. This diverse group of brave warriors was expendable in Westmoreland's pursuit of his goal!

But the small garrison had proven much heartier and more capable than anticipated. They had fought the battle hard, taking numerous casualties, and had won. They had 11 friendly KIA (killed in action)—but recovered over 150 weapons and estimated they had destroyed a regiment and killed over 600.

Nevertheless, the valiant efforts and lives of the small garrison were for naught. This small outpost was robbed of the exhilaration of a battle won, the sweet taste of yesterday's victory fast turning into the bitterness of a political sellout.

In the aftermath of their darkest hour the morning had dawned bright, clear, and crisp, a sharp contrast to the previous morning when fog was so thick that visibility was less than 10 feet. The survivors of yesterday's triumph moved quickly to leave behind the hard-won District Headquarters to the relentless NVA.

Captain (CPT) Bruce Clarke, senior district advisor, was well on his way to earning his Bronze Star as he orchestrated the evacuation of Marines,

Vietnamese, and Montagnards from the smoking compound, which had so recently been a battlefield. CPT Clarke, the leader of the U.S. effort in Khe Sanh village, was filling the role of the new breed of diplomat-soldier, which the Vietnam War had produced—the advisor. Clarke was the advisor to the district chief, CPT Nhi, also a professional soldier, a graduate of Vietnam's West Point. The two were young soldiers equally devoted to Vietnam's freedom. Both a warrior and a humanitarian, Clarke now found himself evacuating the same citizens he had sworn to protect. The same citizens that had fought alongside him and, like him, had experienced that initial ecstasy in victory but had watched that turn to defeat and despair when the Marines of the Khe Sanh Combat Base had demanded they abandon their outpost.

CPT Clarke and his small Army advisory team of four men had spent the best part of 8 months defending and advising the small District Headquarters, but the withdrawal of support from the nearby Combat Base had made the village an easy target and the NVA would soon claim a resounding victory. CPT Clarke knew that this would be the first Government of Vietnam political seat to be lost to the Communists, and it shouldn't happen without a fight. However, abandoned by GEN Westmoreland and COL David Lounds, commanding officer of the 26th Marine Regiment at the Khe Sanh Combat Base, CPT Clarke had no choice but to follow orders and leave behind this small village and its headquarters.

The small contingent of Marines of Combined Action Company OSCAR (CAC-OSCAR), a platoon stationed with CPT Clarke in the village, had been ordered to leave the compound and they left behind a confused and disheartened group of Popular Forces. The Marines had received a radio message some hours earlier from their commander, LT Tom Stamper, telling them to pack up because 8,000–9,000 NVA were headed their way. One of the ammo dumps at the Combat Base had been completely destroyed by incoming artillery. This meant that they could no longer support the village because they were short of ammo. Most of the manned hill positions surrounding the base were under fire. Over 40,000 NVA had surrounded the entire Khe Sanh area and now the Marines were told to consolidate their forces of over 5,000 in order to survive. They were ordered to abandon and withdraw from the village, wounded first.

The armed Popular Forces, the Bru, were not allowed to board the helicopters for evacuation to the Combat Base. The Bru, a Montagnard tribe, had fought alongside their Marine and Army companions, facing the NVA with the same strength, bravery, and determination as any American. Now they were being denied the very freedom for which they had fought. The Marines of CAC-OSCAR were angry about the order to withdraw because the Bru had proved to be extremely loyal throughout the many battles and hardships they'd faced. But they were Marines first and followed orders, even ones with which they disagreed. Now, as the Bru watched the Marines being airlifted from the landing zone they felt as if they had been abandoned. They didn't understand why their comrades had left them to face the enemy alone, especially after they had won such a resounding victory. The frustration and confusion level was high. Cloaking his own disgust and anger, CPT Clarke, his advisors, and the CAC Marines, organized the compound inhabitants so that their evacuation could be as quick and efficient as possible. During the battle the day before air strikes had blown down trees in the coffee plantation close to the District Headquarters. Now the air smelled oddly like morning coffee as CPT Clarke and others scrambled to ensure the safety of the villagers and to get the wounded out as quickly as possible.

Dead NVA bodies and wounded were everywhere and scores of people were pleading to be evacuated. The dead no longer needing him, Sergeant First Class (SFC) Perry's attention was with the wounded waiting anxiously at the landing zone, hoping to find space on the few remaining helicopters that would take them from what 24 hours ago had been hell.

A group of Vietnamese civilians rushed toward the helicopters and in their frenzy to escape the oncoming NVA, grabbed onto the skids of one of the helicopters keeping it from leaving the ground. The departing Marines had to physically push them from the chopper. The explosions from a few M-79 rounds from a Marine grenade launcher into a nearby abandoned tree line caused the frightened Vietnamese to jump back, allowing the helicopter to lift off.

SFC Jim Perry, the medic member of CPT Clarke's advisory team, was busy getting out as many wounded as he could find, packing them into CH-34 helicopters. With smaller bodies, he could get more Bru and Vietnamese civilians into each helicopter. Soon there were would be no more Marine helicopters coming in. He was ordered to get on one of the last Marine helicopters and get out, but he could not leave these wounded people standing on the landing zone. There were still seven or eight wounded Bru and Vietnamese and three of the four young nurses he and the advisory team had trained. One of the nurses, Co Chanh, was clutching her infant to her breast. SFC Perry was beginning to think that he might be stranded there.

With wounded still on the ground SFC Perry now had to find a way to get the rest of the civilians and troops out. Providence provided him one last opportunity. Soon after the last Marine helicopter had departed, an Army of Vietnam (ARVN) CH-34 helicopter appeared in the area, saw them, and landed. After CPT Clarke checked the compound to make sure all of the wounded were accounted for, SFC Perry stuffed the last of them and the nurses into the chopper and climbed aboard himself. He positioned himself so that he could hop off the helicopter if there was too much weight and it could not lift off. But the chopper lifted effortlessly from the ground and he and the other passengers were taken to safety.

Clarke watched with apprehension as the Marines and wounded were lifted off. He was physically exhausted, having been through continual exposure to enemy fire, his own artillery fire, and the tension of sometimes thinking he had fought the battle alone. He and the one remaining member of his advisory team were now alone with the remaining Vietnamese and Bru Forces, numbering about 150 men. The only thing left to do was finish up and that meant getting the forces to the Combat Base. The base was about 5 kilometers away but they would have to take a circuitous route of 8 kilometers to avoid the NVA. Many years later several of the CAC Marines said that CPT Clarke's walking out of the village with the Bru was one of the bravest things they had ever seen—extraordinary heroism and leadership. A West Point graduate, CPT Clarke had learned to take care of his troops first and to lead by example. Walking out with the men who had fought bravely and responded to what he had asked them to do was the only course of action available to him. He didn't consider doing anything else.

Quickly CPT Clarke and SFC King, the last of the American Advisory Team, worked with CPT Nhi, leader of the District Forces, to plan the trek to the Combat Base. Strong NVA forces were still positioned in the area and there was no guarantee they would make it. CPT Clarke walked out of the District Headquarters with his checkbook, his wallet, and all of the weapons and ammunition that he could carry. He didn't even have a hat or helmet on. But he did have 500 rounds of M-16 ammunition, 2 grenades, his Bowie knife, his sawed-off M-79 grenade launcher in a homemade holster, and his .45 caliber pistol. Moving swiftly and stealthily, they traveled through the village, across a stream and then by an indirect route around Hill 471 to the south and west, enabling them to escape the District Headquarters undetected.

As Clarke led the forces to safety he had no idea that the longest siege of the Vietnam War was about to take place and that the assault he and his small band had repulsed had been the first stage of what was to become either a prelude to, or a diversion from, the Tet Offensive. As the only American officer who would fight in Khe Sanh village before the siege, command part of the perimeter at the Combat Base during the siege, and then help plan the relief operations, CPT Clarke would later provide a unique perspective to this defining battle of the Vietnam War. But for now, as they trekked through the humid jungle, tired, frustrated from the confusion of battle, surrounded by smoke, the steady pounding of guns, and the smell of death, CPT Clarke looked out on a valley that at one time had been beautiful, peaceful, and quiet, a valley where once the only sounds were soft winds and birds.

Chapter 2

VIETNAM

Vietnam, a land of richness, of hidden treasures. Shaped like the letter "S," it snakes along the coast of the South China Sea and Pacific Ocean in the eastern part of the Indochina peninsula. Crisscrossed by thousands of streams and rivers—there is a river flowing into the sea every 20 kilometers along the coastline—it is a lush, fluid land with heavy rainfall and a humidity that hangs heavily, almost palpable, in the air. Each season the monsoons sweep across the land, leaving it not clean and refreshed but sodden and thick with red mud that flows like lava. An unforgiving sun burns furiously, causing steam to rise like incense from the ground, and the jungle grows unchecked in exuberant abundance. There is little comfort in cool breezes, small escape from the unrelenting heat.

The jungles sweep up into the mountains and plateaus where a thick double canopy is punctuated with knife-edged elephant grass, tall as a man. Vines rope through the foliage, binding the umbrella of green to the wet tropical ground below. The hot steam of the valleys turns cold and damp here in the mountains. Penetrating. The temperature is chilly and milk white fog moves through the mountains, a barrier to vision. The fog is apocalyptic and wraps the mountains in mystery. The people of the valley don't like the mountains—they fear the bad spirits there.

In spite of constant wars that have deforested this small wet land, the plant life is vibrant and continually revives itself. Dense forests of evergreens and mangroves and rich rain forests are shelter to a number of exotic and endangered species. The Java rhinoceros, the Delacourt and Cat Ba langours, the Asian elephant, the sun bear, the tiger, and the clouded leopard are but a few. Water buffalo and leopards abound, along with monkeys, crocodiles, and lizards. Birds of every color fly the skies and snakes prosper.

With 12,000 plant species and 7,000 species of animals, Vietnam is high on the list of countries with an extensive bio-diversity, but its plant and animal life are only part of its richness. Vietnam has large deposits of oil and gas on its offshore islands and beneath the forests are valuable minerals such as tin, zinc, silver, gold, antimony, precious stones, and coal.

To many, Vietnam may seem a sultry paradise, steeped in the goodness of the earth's bounty, but to others she will always remain a land of bitter conflict and death. Vietnam will always be a cliché for war steeped in controversy, causing domestic turmoil and ending badly. A metaphor for the cloud and confusion of war and politics.

In a war that claimed more than 50,000 American lives there were many battles. But the battle that was the political turning point in the war was Khe Sanh. The North Vietnamese Army (NVA) surrounded the base with at least 20,000 troops and held 6,000 U.S. Marines under siege. In December of 1967 President Johnson, the all-time political operator, had proclaimed that "... all the challenges have been met. The enemy is not beaten, but he knows that he has met his master in the field." The political and military imperative was to make Johnson's boast a reality. But Johnson hadn't counted on the Tet Offensive. On January 31, 1968, the Viet Cong and North Vietnamese troops launched a massive, coordinated, surprise attack on hundreds of targets all across South Vietnam. It was a shocking and unprecedented attack and it inaugurated the war's bloodiest, most widespread fighting, sharply escalating public debate about the value of U.S. actions in Vietnam. Afraid of another Dien Bien Phu, President Johnson felt his career, already in peril over this war, would not recover from this assault. The political mood in the country was swinging against the war and a victory was needed to ensure public support and Lyndon Johnson's political future.

Political pressure and careers in jeopardy would be only a part of the problem of Khe Sanh. A lack of unity of command, friction between commands, and secrecy were all to play a part in the battle. In spite of the efforts of valiant warriors who won the battle of Khe Sanh, the war in Vietnam was lost.

History is a myopic mistress and recites the stories of past wars with an eye to glory and heroism but often blind to fact. However, history is a good teacher, even when myopic, and therefore efforts should be continually made to revisit, rethink, and restructure our future efforts. What Khe Sanh in particular and the Vietnam experience in general, should teach us is not necessarily the critical nature of possessing overwhelming force or the danger of engaging in a global public-relations struggle. It should teach us the importance of military objectives being a clear translation of the conditions that a politician wants for the U.S. military to achieve at the end of a conflict. We owe that to the next generation of brave soldiers, sailors, airmen, and Marines that will endure similar tests of their courage and determination.

Beginning in January of 1968 the people of the United States became gripped by the "Agony of Khe Sanh" as the occupants of the Combat Base in the northwestern corner of South Vietnam began what was to be 77-day siege. The story of the Marines of the Combat Base has been widely reported but it lacks completeness. It is only part of the story. This report will complete the record and in many cases, correct it.

Bob Brewer, the province senior advisor in Quang Tri at the time of the Battle for Khe Sanh village puts the importance of this story clearly in focus: "... actually the big attack, and the biggest ground action in the whole siege of Khe Sanh, took place at Khe Sanh Village, not on the base. And none of that appears in any of the literature. That's the first seat of government that ever fell to the NVA. That's what was so hard."

This account draws on the experiences of the brave men who fought that ground action and through their stories reveals the exhilaration and agony that is war. It was a time of camaraderie, of warriors, of sacrifice and honor. The fight in the village and the subsequent hardships of the Khe Sanh siege changed them all forever. These were common men, whose lives touched each other in so many different ways, enabling them to rise above their individual frailties. They demonstrated a collective courage for the betterment of all.

KHE SANH BEFORE THE BATTLE

Long before the United States occupied Vietnam, the mountainous area that would soon become South Vietnam was peopled by Vietnamese and a native tribe of Montagnards called the Bru. They had lived for generations in thinly disguised tolerance of one another, their relationship tenuous at best. Little love was lost between these two peoples—the mountain people and the valley people. The Bru were the locals; the Vietnamese the new kids on the block. The Vietnamese who had moved into the Huong Hoa district had done so because they could make a better income there than on the coast. They didn't like being in the area but still claimed it as their own. There is arrogance about the Vietnamese and relationships with outsiders are never warm. The Bru viewed the arrival of Asians much as the American Indian viewed the arrival of white men. And much like the American Indian, the Bru was held in low esteem and lived a very meager existence.

The Highlands of Vietnam are home to more than 40 distinct and recognizable aboriginal groups that make up the Montagnard population. The Bru, along with the Bahnar, the Rhade, the Jarai, the Koho, the Sedang and others, once may have numbered 3 million, but have dwindled to only a few hundred thousand. Montagnard (pronounced mountain yard) is a French word meaning mountain people.

In this part of northwest South Vietnam there is only one tribe—the Bru. Their tribe moved nomadically through Laos and North Vietnam. Over time they congregated along Route 9, seeking safety from both the North Vietnamese and American bombers.

The Bru lifestyle is simple and is reminiscent of the lifestyle of native tribes of many countries. They are small in stature with a dark brown skin and thick, coarse black hair. They do not look Asian but Polynesian, and their language has a similar sound to Polynesian languages. They are like all primitive people in that their lives are not complicated and their choices are few. The driving force in their lives is day-to-day survival, and forming close relationships with their environment helps them do that. They have friends and they have enemies. They know good animals and bad animals, benevolent spirits and evil spirits, food that is good and food that is poisonous. There are few shades of gray in the life of the Bru. Their world revolves around small villages where resources are shared and kinship is important. Their leadership is well defined, and moral order is expressed in systems of education and justice that respect individual rights and dignity. They farm the plateaus, the slopes, and the bottomland of ancient rivers. They fish the streams and hunt the forest. Their chief agricultural practice is slash and burn, moving from one place to another in a nomadic fashion, hunting with crossbows and foraging the jungle. They do have cultivated fields, however, and grain rice is grown in extremely small rice paddies along with sticky rice, which is grown on the hillsides. Other crops include corn, peas, coffee, cu-mi, avocado, papaya, pepper, tea, breadfruit, and bananas.

The average Bru family has about seven members. The men marry around the age of 16, while the girls get married around the age of 15. The relationship is monogamous. CPT Nhi places this observation into context. He notes, "Even though most married men have one wife, the Bru were not monogamous. Anha had three wives. I knew this for certain because after evacuating Khe Sanh, Anha's mother, 3 wives and children stayed temporarily with my family living in Quang Tri city at the time."

They live in a house constructed of wood, bamboo, and thatch. The house is on stilts and has two rooms, a small one for cooking and the larger one for sleeping. None of their clothing is self-produced and must be purchased or traded.

They are not traditional Buddhists, as are the Vietnamese, but practice an animistic religion. Spirits dwell in everything. Trees, mountains, streams, birds, snakes, and tigers all have spirits and the laws governing their world are at once esoteric and pragmatic. Consideration and respect for the environment are of paramount importance. For example, one has to be aware of where one relieves oneself. The jungle is not one big outhouse. If you urinate on the wrong shrub, you may contract a great illness. Should you urinate on a tiger (assuming a tiger would allow it), you would curse three generations.

Bru have no training in first-aid procedures and there are no Bru paramedical personnel in the area. Nor will they go to the hospital on their own due, as they mistrust the Vietnamese and lack of resources to pay for treatment and medicine. Common complaints are worms and diarrhea. Malaria, dysentery, malnutrition, TB, and infections are frequent and often go untreated. Soap is nonexistent in the communities as there are not enough funds to buy such luxuries. Clothes are washed without any type of laundry soap. Nutritional diseases are common and infant mortality is high. Babies are usually not named until age two and one-half or three because so many die during the first few years of life. For every ten babies born, seven will die during the first year.

The village of Khe Sanh sat along Highway 9 in the northwestern corner of what used to be South Vietnam. CPT Nhi notes that, "To the older generation of Vietnamese the name of Khe Sanh would always be related to Lao Bao, a famous French prison located near Highway 9 and the Laotian border. The French imprisoned hard-core Vietminh in this fort. The abandoned prison still has rusty chains inside each and every cell."

Khe Sanh was the capital of Huong Hoa district, which was part of Quang Tri province. Huong Hoa is bounded on the north by North Vietnam and on the west and south by Laos. The area is generally mountainous with intermittent streams, heavy undergrowth, and an abundance of wild life. The ridgelines generally run from north to south, perpendicular to the plain which generally runs east west and has in its center Highway 9. The highway was little more than a trail in places.

The area had between 10,000 and 12,000 inhabitants. About 10 percent were Vietnamese who were the merchants and administrators of the district government. They lived entirely in the village of Khe Sanh because they did not like the mountains. The other 90 percent of the population were the Bru, who lived in a series of villages several kilometers off Route 9, but generally in the Khe Sanh plain. There was also the Poillane family who operated a coffee plantation that was south of what would become the Khe Sanh Combat Base. Llinares was another French coffee grower in the district. In addition there was an American family—the Millers—who were working to create a written Bru language and translate the Bible.

The Vietnamese and the Bru were no strangers to conflict and foreign soldiers. Vietnam had been fighting battles for many years, first against the Chinese over many centuries. Then during World War II the clandestine forces of the Office of Strategic Studies (the OSS), which was the precursor to the CIA, engaged the mountain tribes to fight alongside the French against the Japanese. They had fought the Viet Minh with the French during the Indochina war following World War II and now the civil war between the North and South had brought the American military into their midst.

The French had colonized Vietnam during the European quest for colonies early in the twentieth century. Following World War II, the French sought to reestablish their colony. This attempt to assert control of Indochina led to the Indochina war, which ended after the fall of the French Garrison at Dien Bien Phu and the Treaty of Paris. The Treaty of Paris divided the country into two parts: the communist North and the democratic South. The two were divided by a demilitarized zone (DMZ) similar to Korea. The DMZ divided North and South Vietnam—it was rarely, if ever, crossed by U.S. forces on the ground, but often infiltrated by the North Vietnamese.

In July 1962 a detachment of Special Forces arrived in Khe Sanh village and established a security perimeter. At this time there was a civil war in Laos that the CIA was fighting clandestinely using Special Forces. Khe Sanh was strategically located to support, if necessary, that effort In spite of having a tumultuous relationship with the whites during the occupation of the French, the Bru took an instant liking to the newly arrived Special Forces teams.

CPT Nhi remembers that, "During a century of occupation, the French did little, if anything for the Bru. The French missionaries did treat the Bru with respect and dignity, but the rest of the Frenchmen in Vietnam, government officials, military personnel, and plantation owners, treated the Bru as bad as the Vietnamese did. The French policy in Vietnam always was: divide and govern. In carrying out this policy, they played the ethnic card very well. They acted as a protector of the minority—the Bru in this case—against oppressive Vietnamese. A case in point: the French created Nung's territory which was governed by a Nung Colonel named Vong A Sang. The Colonel who as a good man to his people, reported only to the French authority; the government of Vietnam under emperor Bao Dai did not mean a thing to him. The Nung liked the French so much that many young Nungs volunteered to serve in French Armies. My father, a young man at age of 18, volunteered to fight World War II in Europe under the French flag. I believe my father, Hom, Anha and other minorities had the same rosy perception of the French. Yet Anha, my assistant while I was District Chief, could barely read. He could speak French but did not know the alphabet of his own language or the French. This was the literacy that the French left behind for the Bru. Health care was an unfamiliar matter to the Bru. The Bru's labor built Khe Sanh's coffee plantations. What did they get in return? Very little! In my opinion, the French exploited Vietnam and the plantation owners did the same to the Bru." CPT Nhi therefore directly disagrees with the common belief that the Frenchmen that made contact with the Bru beginning with colonial period had treated them with respect and equanimity.

The French had sent missionaries who did good works among the Bru, although they made few converts, and French anthropologists and social workers had given much and treated the Bru with dignity. When Special

Forces teams arrived, they inherited the legacy of good will of the missionaries and harnessed it to serve the needs of counterinsurgency. During the long years of war, a special bond grew between these disparate people: the U.S. Army Special Forces and the Bru.

Before the war many of the Bru worked in the coffee plantations in the area, but absent an ability to export the coffee, there was less demand for their labor. Soldiering became an important source of revenue for the Bru. The young men joined one of the three military forces in the area. The District Popular Forces platoons competed with Lang Vei's Special Forces Camp and its Civilian Irregular Defense Group and the Studies and Observation Group (SOG) elements for personnel. SOG was a clandestine Army Special Forces and CIA effort at gathering intelligence outside of South Vietnam—specifically Cambodia, Laos, and North Vietnam. The patrols would consist of three or more U.S. and about seven mercenary montagnards. They quite often got into huge fights and their casualties were high. Forward Operating Base (FOB) 3 was designed to be a SOG base from which to launch operations into Laos and North Vietnam.

SOG had the best pay and many times waited until one of the other groups had trained the young men and then recruited them away.

In September 1962, Vietnamese engineers built the first airstrip on the plateau, a little on the crude side, but useful. U.S. helicopters and O-1B (Piper Cubs) arrived on station. Not too far away there was an Army of Vietnam (ARVN) Battalion with several Special Forces Advisors at Lang Vei. Two years later, in March of 1964, an O-1B "Bird Dog" was shot down while on a reconnaissance/photo intelligence mission around Khe Sanh. CPT Richard Whiteside, the pilot, became the first American killed at Khe Sanh. The observer, CPT Floyd Thompson, was taken prisoner by the NVA and transported to Hanoi where he became the longest held POW of the Vietnam conflict. That summer the NVA destroyed eight of nine bridges going east along Highway 9 to the coast. A Marine reinforced platoon and Force Recon Team moved into the camp adjacent to the airfield.

Things began to escalate in November when a Special Forces patrol encountered an NVA Company. It was the first confirmed NVA presence in South Vietnam. The following spring in April 1965 Intelligence reported NVA build-up north of Khe Sanh village and around the area of the plateau. The build-up caused concern about security in I Corps, so Special Forces were air lifted onto the plateau to reinforced the defense of the Khe Sanh encampment. Vietnam's provinces were divided into four military regions I–IV Corps, with I Corps in the north and IV Corps south of Saigon in the Mekong Delta. I Corps included four provinces. The U.S. commander of I Corps was also the senior advisor for the region and the commander of the 3rd Marine Amphibious Fleet (III MAF). He commanded almost all of the units in the region, except for some SOG and other special intelligence assets.

From time to time, sporadic fire fights and probes were initiated by the NVA to test the perimeter security. United States and allied forces dug in. The red laterite soil of the Khe Sanh plateau is weathered volcanic rock. In an ironic twist of fate the area's legacy of heat and violent eruptions would continue when the Combat Base was built atop one of five extinct volcanoes that form an arc in Quang Tri province around Tiger Tooth Mountain. The Khe Sanh plateau encampment officially became known as the Khe Sanh Combat Base (KSCB). What was to become the Marine Combat Base, several kilometers north of Khe Sanh village, was important to GEN Westmoreland as a base to launch attacks into Laos to cut the flow of supplies along the Ho Chi Minh trail into the south. The KSCB also provided an anchor to secure the western approaches into Quang Tri province.

Over the next year, things remained pretty quiet in the area. Routine patrols encountered very little activity of the NVA in the area. Khe Sanh village and the plateau remained at ease and relatively peaceful for the most part until June 1966. Intelligence from long-range recon patrols revealed that large numbers of well-armed NVA troops, some Division size, were crossing the DMZ and heading into the South. Khe Sanh became a strategic base because of its location, and it was determined that it must be held if attacked. Reinforcements were airlifted in to supplement the plateau's defense, while perimeter trenches were expanded, and existing bunkers reinforced. In addition, the airstrip on the plateau had to be rebuilt, expanded, and reenforced to handle C-130 cargo planes and to allow for more helicopters and on-call attack aircraft. The face-lift had to occur to insure a direct aerial resupply link to the base. Marine engineers from Fleet Marine Force (FMF) and Navy Sea Bee Construction Battalion 10 began rebuilding, reenforcing, and expanding the airstrip. Even though Intelligence continued to report that more and more well-armed NVA troops were coming across the DMZ, direct contact with any sizable force was extremely minimal, leaving the next 8 months or so as the quiet before the storm.

In late 1966 relations between the Special Forces and Marines began to deteriorate. Marines were used to operating in a "free fire zone" and did not trust the Bru. The Special Forces "A team" moved to Lang Vei and the SOG eventually set up its operations at the "Old French Fort" south of the Combat Base and Route 9 and east of the village of Khe Sanh. Both the SOG and the Special Forces at Lang Vei were based upon the Special Forces basic organization, which contained 10–12-man teams called A teams. These teams were lead by a captain with a first lieutenant as an assistant or executive officer. The noncommissioned officers who made up the team were medical, small arms, demolition, and communications specialists. An A Team was designed to train several hundred local militiamen and turn them into an effective irregular warfare force.

By March 1967 concerns for the defense of Khe Sanh grew as Intelligence reported the NVA were moving toward the Khe Sanh area in large, well-armed numbers. Security was tightened and additional patrols were sent out in all directions, some long range, some short range, to gather information on NVA movements. It was determined that the NVA was grouping for an assault on the plateau, Khe Sanh village, and the outposts. In the spring and early summer of 1967 the Marines fought a series of very bloody battles to secure Hills 861, 881 North, and 881 South. These hills were important because they dominated the northern approaches to the KSCB.

A tragic mistake in the spring of 1967 brought a U.S. Army advisory team to the area. At that time pilots returning from supporting the Marines during the hill fights, or bombing North Vietnam or Laos, would drop their bombs on targets of opportunity rather than try and land with them. For some reason the village of Lang Vei was selected one day as a target of opportunity and 125 Bru civilians were killed and 400 injured. There was a sudden awareness of the plight of the Bru because of the resulting deaths and MAJ James Whitenack and SFC Stan Humphries were deployed to the area on short notice to establish an advisory team and to assist in the distribution of aid and assistance to the Bru.

Chapter 3

DISTRICT HEADQUARTERS

The "friendly bombing" of the Bru villagers brought an immediate reaction from the I Corps Commander in Danang, Lieutenant General (LTG) Cushman. The Bru were an important source of manpower for both the Civilian Irregular Defense Group (CIDG) who manned the camp at Lang Vei, and the Studies and Observation Group (SOG), and it was important that the recruiting base be maintained. There were over 10,000 Bru in the area and more than 10 percent of them were on government payrolls as soldiers of one kind or another. The American forces could not let these people become supporters of the NVA, so Cushman established an advisory team to coordinate and supervise the distribution of aid to the Bru within the Huong Hoa district, which included Khe Sanh. And despite the political motivation, there was a humanitarian element to this effort.

A district could be called an equivalent of our county government and the province would be an equivalent of a state government. An ARVN colonel commanded each province and a district chief, usually an ARVN major, commanded each district. The Huong Hoa district government was a combination of military and civilian, American and Vietnamese.

The District Advisory Team reported to the Province Advisory Team in Quang Tri (a combination of American civilian and military), which in turn reported to the 1st ARVN Infantry Division advisor in Hue (American military advisor to the senior ARVN command in the area). He reported to the I Corps Commander (American military) in Danang. This was a unique situation because the province senior advisor, Bob Brewer, was an American civilian and had a separate chain of command because he worked for the CIA. A former Airborne soldier, he was now a CIA operative serving as the province senior advisor. To maintain military presence in the chain of command, Brewer's deputy was Army LTC Joe Seymoe. LTC Seymoe was the deputy province advisor and Brewer's primary military advisor. Brewer was a crucial participant in all military and political decisions that were made in this province bordering North Vietnam and Laos. His presence reflected the critical nature of intelligence concerning events north of the Demilitarized Zone (DMZ) between North and South Vietnam.

The District Advisory Team, made up of U.S. Army personnel, would be headquartered in the village of Khe Sanh with the Huong Hoa district chief and subsector commander, Lieutenant (LT) Tinh-A-Nhi. The district chief's area of responsibility included the village of Khe Sanh and the Khe Sanh Combat Base (KSCB), Lang Vei and the entire northwest section of South Vietnam. As the district chief, he was the political administrator of the area and supervised the police, medical services, etc. As subsector commander, LT Nhi, an ARVN first lieutenant, was responsible for all Vietnamese military in the area except for those working with the Army Special Forces. He commanded eight Bru Popular Forces (PF) platoons and one under-strength Regional Force (RF) (Vietnamese militia) company. South Vietnam had local forces for point and regional defense in addition to its regular forces. These were of two types:

1. The PFs who were organized in platoons and normally were used to defend their own village or a bridge or other site near their own village.
2. RFs who were organized in Companies and were used for small regional missions.

The PFs usually were under the command of the village chief and district chief while the RFs were under the command of the province chief who would and did second them for missions to the district chiefs. The PFs were the most poorly paid, trained, and equipped of all Vietnamese forces. The RFs and PFs came to be known by U.S. troops as "Rough Puffs."

LT Nhi's wife and son remained in Saigon while he performed his duties in Khe Sanh. The common wisdom that has been published several places is that the district chief was a political and military position and LT Nhi was there to reverse what started off as a politically disastrous career. Others in the same position in other districts were majors but because of his politics he had not yet made the grade. One of the first Nung (Vietnamese of Chinese origin) to graduate from Dalat, Vietnam's West Point, he had been "exiled" to this mountainous area because he had supported the "wrong side" during one of the Buddhist uprisings. Now he was based in this remote mountain outpost, strategically removed from any possibility, it was thought, of critical military responsibility. CPT Nhi contradicts this and puts his entire career into another perspective. He notes that,

Although many officers' careers were ruined by their connections with the Buddhists, for me that wasn't the case. I was a Confucian, not a Buddhist, and although I had sympathy for the Buddhist's cause, I didn't express it in word or deeds. I was picked to be Huong Hoa District chief among two other officers. LT Vu Van Phao, my classmate and a Captain. In brief, I did not feel 'exiled'. On the contrary I was proud of the assignment.

As a Dalat graduate I, and many of my classmates, had taken on an ambitious mission. We sought to be military leaders, from battalion commanders to chief of the armed forces. As professional soldiers, we had no desire to be involved in politics but rather to revolutionize the ARVN step by step as we were promoted to higher positions. Many of the upper-class Dalat graduates had taken over command of Brigades and Regiments and one third of the battalion commanders of regular forces were Dalat graduates. When I was based in this remote mountain outpost, assigned to be Huong Hoa District chief, it was a posting that I was quite proud of. (I myself was informed by the G1 officer of the ARVN General Staff of a promotion to Lieutenant Colonel on May 1, 1975. Unfortunately it was one day late: the South Vietnam government collapsed one day earlier. This promotion wouldn't come to me as a surprise at all because I had been a major since late 1970.)

The District Compound was in the village of Khe Sanh and had several distinct parts. In the southwestern corner was a fort that was left over from the French days. The walls were of pierced steel planking (PSP) with about 18 inches of packed Khe Sanh red clay in between. The fort was triangular in shape and had a punji stake-filled moat surrounding it. A pagoda was not more than 25 meters outside of the barbed-wire bound compound on the west. The area behind the pagoda led directly to the seam between the French Fort and the main compound. The pagoda was a sturdy building made of concrete with decorative stucco on the inside and outside. Behind it was a narrow path that ran north and south and was bordered with trees. The tree-lined path reminded one of the trails in the Normandy "bocage" area— small fields separated by trees and hedges and sunken roads that caused the allied forces so much difficulty in breaking out of Normandy during World War II.

On the north was the main gate to the compound and part of the village. Immediately across the street was a restaurant, euphemistically called the "Howard Johnson's," which did a rather brisk business with the military personnel. The eastern edge of the compound included vehicle shelters and then the village. The police station and local dispensary were only 100 meters away on the east.

Completing the circle on the south and southeastern side of the compound was the landing zone (LZ). The LZ had the warehouse to the east, the CAC Marines to the north, the old French fort to the west and an old French minefield to the south. The minefield was overgrown and the number of mines that might be in there was unknown. Efforts to burn the area off had had only marginal results and no detonations. Beyond it was a small coffee plantation that extended along the entire southern flank of the compound.

Another major player in the area was the U.S. Army Special Forces Studies and Observations Group contingent that was initially located in an upstairs room in the building west and north from the District Headquarters. Later they relocated to the Old French Fort that overlooked Route 9 near the road that lead to the Combat Base and which protected the eastern approaches to the village.

The headquarters of the CAC and it's 1st Platoon, CAC-OSCAR 1, were also in the District Compound. The company was commanded by LT Stamper, a combat veteran of too many Vietnamese battles. The 1st Combined Action Platoon (CAP) called OSCAR 1 was made up of a Marine rifle squad and a platoon of Bru PFs. On January 21, 1968, it was led by Sergeant (SGT) John Balanco.

The Khe Sanh Combat Base was located due north of the village about five straight-line distance kilometers. In the spring and summer of 1967 the base had one Marine infantry battalion and the equivalent of an artillery battalion, plus assorted combat service support troops to operate the facilities, run the airfield, and maintain the few helicopters that were kept there. The base provided medical support to the surrounding military installations and was commanded by COL David Lounds. A veteran of WW II, Lounds had served in Korea and the Dominican Republic before becoming the regimental commander of the 26th Marine Regiment in Khe Sanh in July 1967. Initially COL Lounds only had one battalion of the 26th Marines at Khe Sanh. However, during the days right before the attack on the village the other battalions were added as was the 9th Marines to complete the four battalions of Marines that were at the base during siege of the combat base.

Also located in the District Compound was a two-man element from the Joint Technical Advisory Detachment (JTAD). Their cover story was that they were drawing maps of the area for National Geographic. They used a light blue truck at Khe Sanh with a STP sticker on the side door. The team was composed of LT James Taronji and a SGT George Amos who wore Warrant Officer (WO) Insignia. CAC-OSCAR provided logistical support for them. Allegedly, they were feeding false information through the police chief to the North Vietnamese. George Amos later told his wife Delores

"I've been, as you know, on a short but very important mission to Khe Sanh, Vietnam. I lived in a tent surrounded by a squad (12) Marines and a company of 150 South Vietnamese and Montagnard troops. I was there because we were getting information about the North Vietnamese Army (NVA) units in the area."

All of these disparate groups responded to different headquarters. The advisory team responded to the Province Advisory Team headed by Bob Brewer in Quang Tri. CPT Frank Willoughby and his Special Forces A Team at the Lang Vei Special Forces Camp with the CIDG and Bru soldiers responded to 5th Special Forces Group in Danang. SOG, which operated from the Old French Fort, responded to a Headquarters in Danang, which, in turn responded to SOG in Saigon. CAC-OSCAR responded to COL Lounds at the Combat Base, as the senior Marine in the area. The 26th Marines at the Khe Sanh Combat Base were part of the 3rd Marine Division headquartered in Dong Ha and received orders from that area.

That confusion and struggle was mirrored on a smaller scale inside the District Headquarters. The Marines in CAC-OSCAR 1 thought that all of the PFs were under their command and control while the army advisors understood them to be part of the District Forces under the district chief—LT Tinh-A-Nhi. LT Nhi traditionally sided with the army advisors because they could provide him resources. There was usually a lack of coordination on operations, unless the district chief himself was involved. The Marines would go out on patrols that only they knew about, leaving the Advisory Team to guess at their probable motivation or tactical objectives. This resulted in a tenuous unity of command situation, shored up however by a friendly coexistence brought about by close quarters and the affinity of Americans for working together. It was neither the best of circumstances, nor the tight-knit machine it could have been, but it was adequate.

In addition to the day-to-day operations of each command, there were logistical problems that affected all groups equally. Situated in the mountains with poor roads, accessibility from outside the province was very poor. In July of 1967 there was an attempt to move 175 MM self-propelled guns from Dong Ha to Khe Sanh. The extended range of these guns would have allowed them to reach to Co Roc Mountain across the border in Laos and beyond. Due to their weight, the guns had to be moved overland along Route 9. On the 63-kilometer stretch of Route 9 between Khe Sanh village and Dong Ha, there were 36 crumbling, washed out, or destroyed bridges. Throughout the summer attempts to move the 175s and resupply the Combat Base over this land route failed due to the road conditions, and the presence of numerous North Vietnamese ambushes. The 175s remained at a fire base supporting the action along the DMZ called the Rockpile. Following those failures the Marines gave up on the concept of vehicle convoys to Khe Sanh and elected to resupply by air. Coordination of these efforts was often slowed or impossible due to miscommunication among the groups.

Multiple tactical problems and situations should have called for a united effort across the broad range of military groups, but that was not the case. The theorists of warfare believe that unity of command will lead to focus and unity of effort in pursuit of the unit's objectives. Without unity of command at all levels of command, however, there were multiple and diverging objectives on the part of the units on the Khe Sanh plateau. The Marines at the Combat Base were looking for GEN Westmoreland's set-piece firepower-intensive battle. They wanted the Special Forces and advisors out of the way. The advisors' principal mission was to care for the Bru, and the other two Army units' major emphasis was patrolling to generate intelligence for analysis and subsequent dissemination in Danang and Saigon. The lack of unity of command therefore had each of the units pursuing its own objectives without anyone synchronizing their efforts toward a broader goal. The objectives were often divergent in nature. Unity of command did not really exist even at I Corps [III Marine Amphibious Force (MAF)] because the Special Forces were in a different chain of command. The absence of unity of focus (command) played a significant role in the loss of lives, loss of political ground, and the losing of the war.

THE VILLAGE PARTICIPANTS

The U.S. Marine Corps frequently had a very strong presence in the Huong Hoa province, with the majority of them in the traditional main line formation role—Marines focused on fighting the NVA. These Marines were not involved with civic action but in eliminating enemy and securing terrain. During the period 1966 onward the Khe Sanh Combat Base was occupied by a force as small as a battalion with some artillery and other types of reinforcements. However, when significant NVA forces were detected in the area additional Marines would be brought in to dislodge them. Once this was done the Marines would relocate to other areas to seek out and destroy the NVA. The "hill fights" of the spring of 1967 are a classic example of this tactic.

Following the hill fights, CAC "O" was established when the 3rd Marines who had been at the combat base departed the area. The idea was for the Marines to train the PFs, the indigenous tribe of Bru, to make them a much more credible fighting force. The PFs, when they were on duty, trained and lived in the District Headquarters bunkers with the Marines. On January 21, 1968, the 1st Platoon was led by a district newcomer, SGT John Balanco.

CAC was created to offset the desire of the U.S. military to transform the war into the more comfortable and familiar war they had known in World War II and Korea. Whenever possible *the people*, the rural civilians of Vietnam, were brushed aside, abandoned, evacuated, or ignored so that

U.S. combat forces could strike at large units of the main force Viet Cong
and NVA.

Expressing the views of many military and civilian leaders, undersec-
retary of state Nicholas Katzenbach observed in June 1967 that the war
of attrition against the Viet Cong main force units and the NVA was "the
key," and that the United States should "recognize that pacification is not
the ultimate answer—we have neither the time nor the manpower."

Within the Marines there was a dissenting voice—LTC William R. Corson. The first Combined Action Commander explains the birth of the CAC
concept and the shoestring that it operated on in the following paragraphs.

The inability to get Westmoreland, McNamara, and LBJ to focus on the
strategic realities in Vietnam drove the concept for the CAP program, which
we finally adopted. Two practical points were involved:

One, there was no way the Marine Corps, here read that to include
Walt, Krulak, Greene, and later Nickerson, could establish an official authorized, full TO&E organization called a CAP Program. In the face of
COMUSMACV's adamant opposition to the CAP concept, control over
the flow of personnel to Vietnam and force levels, as well as designated
units, was vested in the ASD for Systems Analysis. Thus, if the Marine
Corps wanted a CAP program, it would have to be created out of the
hide of our authorized TO&E units. This was done, and I was carefully
admonished not to stir up, or draw undue attention to, the pot by beg-
ging too briskly for CAP Marines from my classmates, peers, etc. It was
my task to convince my friends that it was in their and their unit's best
interests to support the CAP effort with able troops. I might add that I
found out who among my "friends" were willing to subordinate their own
ambitions to the security needs of their troops and those of the Vietnamese
in their Tactical Areas of Responsibility by giving up some of their Marines
to the barely proven CAP concepts we had tested in the Southern Sector
Command. There was no time to try and replicate those experiments to
determine their applicability throughout I Corps. The deteriorating tactical
situation dictated that we had to go with what we had learned and, with
confidence in the ingenuity and integrity of the individual Marine; we set
forth on an interesting journey.

The other practical point involved that of "beans and bullets." As all
of you know so well, Marines in Vietnam were not embarrassed by riches
in terms of the logistical requirements. Both General Walt and Nickerson
looked the other way as we begged, borrowed, and stole from the Army,
Navy, and Air Force to enable our CAPs to function. Out of this effort
emerged what was called the "Danang Mafia." Although midnight requi-
sitions have long been a part of the Marine Corps way of doing business,
I must say that the officers and Senior Non-Commissioned Officers in the

CAP headquarters raised that tradition to a new and higher standard, or "take." Also, I should acknowledge the monumental contribution of a classmate, and a former comrade in the Korean War, who had become a supply officer in the interim between Korea and Vietnam. As you may know, a number of regular line officers were ordered to a special duty or communications officer tours during that period. My friend chose to forsake his line military occupational specialty and go supply after completing his forced tour. When he hit Vietnam he was placed in charge of the Machine Records element. In this role he pilfered and provided me with an excess of 5,000 blank MR cards which enabled us to requisition a wide variety of material under several (non-Marine Corps) fake unit designations.

We broke every rule in the logistical book, and Lew Walt (Commandant of the Marine Corps) never even blinked when he visited a specially exposed CAP and saw light and heavy mortars, as well as 50 caliber machine guns in the hamlet. He also never blinked when he saw eleven year old Vietnamese children armed with M-2 carbines, provided by our friends in the USN, helping in the defense of their hamlet. A fact that was based on an act of deliberate insubordination on my part whereby I elected to arm the Vietnamese civilians in direct violation of COMUSMACV orders. The Vietnamese "people," i.e., those we were expected to protect in the hamlets, were considered to be unreliable and the weapons would "fall into the hands of the Communists." That was nonsense. None of the weapons we provided the Vietnamese people, to help provide for their common defense, ever turned up in the hands of Communists. The Danang Mafia also "liberated" 12X12 lumber from the USAF which saved Marine lives and helped the CAPs to defend their hamlets by providing them with much needed essential overhead cover during the TET offensive. This wasn't "stealing" because according to McNamara's automated Department of Defense supply system, there were no 12X12s in-country. They were on "back order."

In their bases around Chu Lai, near the border of Quang Ngai and Quang Tin provinces, around Danang and Hue; and later farther north and west toward the DMZ and Khe Sanh, the Marines established CAP, rifle squads stationed for indefinite periods in villages, where they worked as part of a team composed of the Marine squad and a PF Platoon. The CAP's mission was to identify and root out the Viet Cong shadow government within the village, win the support of the people, protect them from Viet Cong coercion, train and encourage the PFs, collect local intelligence, and participate in various local self-help projects referred to as "civic action." The 13-man squad, usually commanded by a sergeant in his early twenties, operated with a degree of autonomy and isolation unusual in Vietnam, or indeed in any military organization. Except for brief visits by the CAC commander and a resupply truck or helicopter, the CAP was alone; absorbed within the daily routine of village life. "Women sweep and cook, children play, the farmers work the fields or sit and talk, the sun beats down and the bugs bite."

LTC Corson concludes with some comments on the role of CAPs and their success in denying the Viet Cong and NVA areas to safely operate in.

Pacification includes a number of processes. However, it is not defined simply as a process. A better term is that it is descriptive of a condition. In the case of the hamlets in South Vietnam, it was the belief and perception of the Vietnamese people that they were safe in their own homes. This idea, or feeling of safety, was the sine qua non without which there was no "pacification purpose," or potential gain, simply by providing the humanitarian assistance that the indigenous government had never provided. The CAP Marines, by virtue of their willingness to stand and die to protect the Vietnamese from their twin enemies, i.e., the Communists and the GVN [South Vietnamese Government] made believers out of the Vietnamese peasants. Once that had occurred, the hamlet had been "pacified." In one very important sense, this speaks to the people's "state of mind." If the people's state of mind was such that they believed they were safe, or at least would be protected, the essential condition to proceed with visible pacification/rehabilitation efforts was in hand and in place. Without it, everything was just too much dross. I can't emphasize too strongly that the desired state of mind had to be achieved first. Parenthetically, I observed on many occasions following a heavy VC attack which had been finally beaten off after a toll of lives and physical destruction, a spirit of unity between the CAP Marines and the people as they set about the task of rebuilding the hamlet and getting ready for the next attack or problem. In sum, security and its acquisition is not simply the erection of barricades.

COL Lounds and GEN Westmoreland it would seem did not understand this.

Another CAP, OSCAR 2, was between 250 and 350 meters west of the District Compound along Highway 9 in its own little compound. CAP OSCAR 2 partially protected the District Headquarters from attacks from the west along the highway. However, it was possible for the enemy to infiltrate between OSCAR 2 and the District Headquarters.

Between OSCAR 1 and 2 there were approximately 24 Marines in the compound area. The advisory team came late into the mix. Major (MAJ) James Whitenack, from Brooklyn, New York, was transferred in November of 1967, after a short stint in the Headquarters Commandant's office of III MAF, to Khe Sanh to be the district advisor. An enlisted Korean War veteran, he had returned to the Army to attend Officers Candidate School at Fort Benning. In 1960 he became the aide-de-camp to the deputy commanding general of 3rd Army in Europe. The draw down of officers from Germany to fill units in Vietnam resulted in him occupying many administrative positions in a brigade headquarters before going to Vietnam. Upon arrival in Vietnam he was picked to become the district advisor in Khe Sanh. He had no experience in district advising, had no formal training, but he was available, he was a major and he was in the infantry.

Major Whitenack recalls:

I arrived in Saigon in mid December 1966. Processed in and assigned to Advisory Team 1, I Corps Advisory Group, Danang. The Non-Commissioned Officer (NCO) who was my seatmate on the flight over became the NCO in charge of the Enlisted/NCO Club in Danang. That was my source of beer that we drank in lieu of the chemically treated water that we had. We rotated turns getting the water from the Combat Base between the SOG guys that were in the building across from our compound.

When SOG initially came to Khe Sanh the several Special forces officers lived at "Howard Johnson's" (the name given to the Vietnamese restaurant across the street from the District Headquarters). Later, as they recruited montagnards to take part in their cross-border missions, they needed more space and moved to the "old French Fort," which was less than a kilometer east of the District headquarters and just off the access road to the combat base. Subsequently SOG moved to the combat base where they were to build a Forward Operating Base (FOB) known as FOB-3. It was built as an appendage onto the Khe Sanh Combat Base, with its own gate and perimeter to secure.

I was in Danang until 6 March 1967, and then Sergeant First Class Humphries and myself were told to open the sub-sector in Khe Sanh. We flew out in a Huey and were dropped off at the 'helipad.' We had our clothes, one case of C-Rations, a PRC-25 radio, M-1 carbines and 2 clips of ammo. We ultimately replaced our carbines with M-16's obtained at the Khe Sanh Combat Base (KSCB). We were a little out of range with our radio. Locally we were okay, but we could not talk to Quang Tri. I did scrounge up a 292 antenna and that helped out a bit. We could talk to Quang Tri at night and sometimes during the day. Communications with our parent headquarters were intermittent at best.

I didn't have any trouble getting things flown up to us, as I had made friends with many of the C-123 and C-130 pilots that flew from Danang to Khe Sanh. You can make a lot of friends with the pilots by giving them an AK-47. They didn't like flying with only a pistol if they went down. They also flew up all the wire, sandbags, etc. that we were able to beg, borrow or steal. They also flew up the jeep that I acquired. Before that, if memory serves me right, the only transportation we had was the district 3/4 ton truck.

The advisory team initially located in a small room next to LT Nhi's office. Later, when the police moved into the village, the advisors were given the two-room "suite" at the western edge of the District Headquarters and quickly made the place habitable. MAJ Whitenack and SFC Humphries began the task of advising and procuring aide for the district's villages, working hand in hand with LT Nhi.

Throughout the time MAJ Whitenack was in command there were a number of military movements and operations in the Khe Sanh area. On April 24, 1967, Bravo Company, 1st Battalion, 9th Marines, encountered and engaged a large, well-armed NVA force, estimated to be battalion strength, headed for Khe Sanh. Heavy fighting continued through the afternoon, and even though the Marines were out-numbered, they carried the day. Intelligence determined that the 1st Battalion had caught the NVA by surprise, causing an unorganized, premature counterattack against the 1st Marines just north of Hill 861. The area around Khe Sanh now seemed infested with NVA. Over the next 3 days, the 2nd Battalion, 3rd Marines and 3rd Battalion, 3rd Marines, along with support personnel, were airlifted into Khe Sanh to re-enforce the perimeter to stop the NVA drive toward the plateau. They operated under the command of 26th Marine Commander who was the commander of the Combat Base. During the movement of units in and out of KSCB units would come and go depending upon their availability while the command element for the region and the base was provided by the 26th Marine Regimental Headquarters.

Over the next 2 weeks, fighting in the hills intensified as the 3rd Marines fought to seize three key hills near the Khe Sanh Fire Base. After extremely concentrated prep fire from artillery and air support, the 2nd Battalion assaulted the slopes of Hill 861 under ground fire from well armed and entrenched NVA, but managed to seize the first objective, Hill 861. With the hill secured, the 2nd Battalion was airlifted back to the encampment for re-supply, and then was airlifted to the area around Hill 881N. Coinciding with the 2nd Battalions attack on Hill 861, the 3rd Battalion's assaulted Hill 881S, but the prep fire on this hill had little to no effect on the entrenched NVA who were well armed, and a much larger force than that on Hill 861. After 4 days of alternating prep fire from artillery and air, napalm drops, bombing runs, and numerous assaults on the hill, the 3rd Battalion finally seized control of the second objective, Hill 881S.

Having minimal to no rest, the 2nd Battalion encountered and engaged, on the morning of the May 3, a heavily armed NVA company-sized force and dug in. Over the next couple of days, the 2nd Battalion turned back multiple, extremely strong counterattacks by the NVA a little south of Hill 881N. Regrouping, the 2nd Battalion on May 5, assaulted and seized control of the third objective, Hill 881N. By May 11, intelligence reported a major decline in NVA activity around the Khe Sanh area, with only minimal contact. Intelligence analysts believed the NVA had retreated north to resupply and regroup, but also believed that they intended on returning, next time in larger, better-armed numbers. Khe Sanh remained on full alert but the hill fights were over. The Marines from the Khe Sanh Combat Base declared that all of their objectives had been achieved. After an interval the 3rd Marines were redeployed for action elsewhere.

Meanwhile, it was not a quiet time at the Khe Sanh District Headquarters. MAJ Whitenack continues:

> Our team got bigger with the arrival of Specialist Gerhke, who was to be our radioman. SFC Jim Perry who was our medic came from Walter Reed Army Hospital in Washington, where he had worked in the operating room. He treated several Bru and Regional Force soldiers from the triangular fort in our rear when we were attacked in May/June.
>
> The Viet Cong and NVA came from the southwest. The largest weapons the regional forces had were a 60mm mortar, machine-guns and small arms. At that time "spooky" (C-47 gunship) would fly out of Danang and fly north to the DMZ, then turn south down to the border between I Corps and II Corps. Just our luck, the C-47 (spooky) was in his southern leg. Took a bit of time for him to get to us, but when he did, he really hosed them down and things turned calm again. Most of the bodies were carried off-but we still had a body count.

The District Advisory Team conducted squad (10–12 man) and platoon (30–40 man) sized patrols weekly, covering areas east of the old French fort and the road going up to the Combat Base. They also went west to the Lang Vei Special Forces (SF) camp and south and southwest of the town.

MAJ Whitenack continues:

> In the first week of May (5th or 6th I think) while monitoring the radios, I was listening to the action going on at Lang Vei Special Forces camp. I knew they were under attack when I heard one of the SF "guys" say I am the last American alive. We were already on alert, so in the pre dawn hours we saddled up to get over to the camp ASAP. I proceeded in my jeep along with Humphries, Perry and Gerhke, to be followed on foot by LT Nhi (the district chief) and regional force troops.
>
> We threw caution to the wind and raced into the camp not knowing what to expect. I found SFC Steptoe alive along with two other Americans who had been in the communications (commo) bunker during the attack. That bunker was set on fire by rockets and satchel charges. It seems that when the commo bunker caught fire they crawled out and hid in a communications trench. I found them when I entered the camp. The enemy was aided by VC/NVA infiltrators recruited into the Civilian Irregular Defense Group (CIDG). These "recruits" had cut the barbed wire on the south slope of the hill and put pegs in the ground through the minefield. This allowed

the NVA to enter the camp, get to the camp sector where the Americans were and launch their attack. They hit Captain (CPT) Crenshaw's bunker with a B-40 rocket. When he was staggering out, they hit him with a burst of AK-47 fire. Seconds later, LT Stallings (had radio watch that night) came out of the mess hall and was also killed by AK-47 fire. The VC already in the camp at the same time went around the perimeter throwing satchel charges into the bunkers. Let me tell you, it was a mess at first light. Tragically, it was Crenshaw's first or second day in command.

Sergeant Perry had been doing what he could for the wounded, however shortly thereafter, all kinds of Special Forces brass, medics, etc. arrived and we backed off.

After this incident, the Special Forces moved and established a new camp approximately 800 meters to the west. The "new" Lang Vei camp was 5–8 kilometers from Khe Sanh village. After the initial attack on Lang Vei, the South Vietnamese Provincial government decided to move all the inhabitants into Vietnamese-controlled areas around Quang Tri. LT Nhi and Major Whitenack arranged for truck transport. They drove out to the Sepone (Tcepone) River, which is on the border between Laos and Vietnam, loaded up everyone who lived between the river and Khe Sanh village and transported the Vietnamese to Dong Ha, right down the road from Quang Tri. The abandoned villages were burned. Anything that could not be moved was destroyed. This denied the NVA and the Viet Cong any food, lodging, laborers, etc. along the Laotian border. In essence it became a free-fire zone.

MAJ Whitenack's advisory team continued to grow:

Staff Sergeant King was the next to arrive. This filled out our team with the exception of my Assistant District Advisor. At this time Advisory Team One had Australian Warrant Officers (WOs) serving as Assistant District Advisors. These WOs were outstanding; however, I was assigned an Australian WO that had emigrated from Germany and was worthless. He was replaced and Lieutenant (LT) Bruce Clarke was assigned. At that point we had a fully qualified operational team.

In August 1967, LT Bruce Clarke, newly arrived to Vietnam from commanding an airborne cavalry troop in Germany, joined the District Advisory Team in Khe Sanh village.

The role of advisor is a delicate billet and one that requires not only political expertise but also a genuine comprehension of the vagaries and nuances of counterinsurgency. LT Clarke arrived in Vietnam after in-depth studies on the subject at the Special Warfare Center at Fort Bragg. He was an idealist and thought that advisory-type duty would be the future of the U.S. Army. While at West Point, Clarke had studied warfare and counterinsurgency and was convinced that it was the warfare of the future.

A West Point graduate, Clarke had followed in his father's footsteps at the academy. Clarke's father had earned two Distinguished Service Crosses during the airborne assault on Sicily in July 1943. It was there that he was killed in action, so to the young Bruce Clarke, LTC Arthur F Gorham was only a man in a scrapbook. When his mother remarried in February 1945, Ed Clarke adopted Bruce. Ed was to be the only father that he knew, but he encouraged Bruce to know his father's heroism and to go to West Point. After graduation from West Point, LT Clarke went to Airborne and Ranger schools.

His first assignment had been as a platoon leader in an armored cavalry squadron in Germany. He later assumed command of the only Airborne/ Cavalry troop in Europe and honed his leadership and warrior skills as he took young recruits and melded them into a 160-man combat team. But his real interest lay in the political/military interaction that was required of an advisor and he volunteered to go to Vietnam in that capacity.

Chapter 4

DAY-TO-DAY OPERATIONS OF THE ADVISORY TEAM

In one of his first letters home to his parents, dated August 14, 1967, LT Clarke described the Huong Hoa district, the plight of the Bru and the Khe Sanh area:

> I have been on the job now for about 10 days. Just to ease your minds I haven't had a VC round fired at me yet nor have I fired a round. Saturday night the Marines shook us up a little bit. About 2300 we were sitting playing hearts when an arty round went off very near our compound. After 30 seconds of pandemonium we were all in our bunkers awaiting the attack. As it turned out the Marines were firing some harassing fire and had the wrong data on their guns.
>
> The terrain here is very rolling and wooded. There are coffee plantations around and a Marine Base about 8 miles away. That's where we get our supplies, etc. Except for the people in Khe Sanh village, the people are all Montagnards of the Bru tribe (pronounced Brew). They are a nomadic people who live by slash and burn. They cut and burn an area and plant their crops and then when the land gives out they move away. Right now they are centered around the area of Khe Sanh because the VC and NVA were giving them such a hard time. They are a very poor people. We give a bag of bulgur, one of corn and a gallon of salad oil to 476 families each month, but this is not enough.

What they need is agriculture of their own. Their staple is rice, but this is not a rice producing area so they pay exorbitant prices for that rice that comes in over Highway 9. Their sanitation and health are my major projects.

Right now I'm trying to figure out how to get a market economy started. We need help for them. The big thing that we need is decent transportation to market the crossbows and flutes that some of the people make and to bring in rice more cheaply. If anyone at the churches, etc. want to "adopt" a village just let me know and I'll send them the particulars.

The advisors spent most of their time visiting the different villages and working with the village chiefs to improve the lot of the people. Doc Perry and the nurses that he had trained conducted numerous medical visits, known as MEDCCAP (Medical-Civil Action Program) visits to different villages. There was a school built for the Bru children and a midwife was established in the village to aid in childbirth. Each month bulgur and oil were distributed by the district chief to the villagers and the advisors went on each of these missions to insure a proper and equitable distribution of provisions. As the aid work progressed SGT Humphries, and later SGT King, continued trying to improve the quality of the PF's training.

Because of the inaccessibility of the area, supplies were a problem. Resupply trips were frequent. Every day LT Clarke or MAJ Whitenack went to the Combat Base to fill up several 5-gallon water cans that the advisors had for drinking water and to see if there was any new intelligence. They also stopped at FOB-3 or the Old French Fort to chat with the Special Forces folks there. About once a week a coordination meeting with the Special Forces at Lang Vei occurred.

The advisory team frequently sent members to Danang to trade Bru-made crossbows for supplies and other items that the Bru needed. Agency for International Development's (AID) supplies for the Bru also came by air from Danang and were stored in a warehouse that was on the southeastern corner of the District Compound.

When the advisors would go on their trips around the area Sergeant Major Hom, the Bru PF senior noncommissioned officer, would send one or two PFs for security. He often would go himself. Hom had served with the French and spoke better French than Vietnamese. LT Clarke used French to communicate with him and SFC King was learning to speak Bru, which was very helpful. Hom was a legend among the Bru because he had fought with the French and survived. It was interesting to observe what weapon he would carry. One could tell how much of a threat Hom thought that there was in the area, based upon his weapon of choice. A Browning Automatic Rifle meant a high threat level, a Thompson submachine-gun was a slightly less threat and his trusty M-1 rifle with its rope sling indicated a normal situation.

Each week someone from the District Advisory Team went to Quang Tri for the weekly Advisory Team 4 coordination meeting and resupply trip. Air America provided a helicopter for this trip. Sodas, beer, and other staples would be brought back. The advisors often "loaned" beer to the two Special Forces units. The coordination on such items helped make the three Army elements closer. Often a case of whisky would be bought and traded to the Seabees at the Combat Base for fresh meat, eggs, and vegetables (the Seabees ran the Marine food storage reefers). LT Nhi was fond of Salem cigarettes and quite often someone on a resupply trip was able to procure those for him. This was a source of debate within the advisory team. MAJ Whitenack did not want to let any "contraband" into the area and would regularly "shake down" Vietnamese who were returning from the coast. He did not trust the Vietnamese and if an aircraft came in that might have Vietnamese on it he'd go out and check them for contraband; specifically he was looking for black market cigarettes. This created a bit of animosity and distrust between the advisory team and the Vietnamese forces and local merchants. LT Clarke felt that a few cigarettes were worth the price of support from the local officials and looked the other way. He would even occasionally buy Nhi cigarettes. Because of this attitude and approach, Nhi and Clarke worked better together when the going got rough.

James (Doc) Perry was a SFC and the Military Assistance Command Vietnam (MACV) senior medical advisor for the Huong Hoa district, Khe Sanh area. Doc Perry had been in the Army for over 10 years by the time he arrived in Khe Sanh. After a brief stint in the Navy from 1952 to 1955 he had attended the Great Lakes College of Physical Medicine and had channeled that interest into the Army medical field. His specialty was emergency medicine and he was trained to "set up shop" anywhere, especially in areas with no doctors, nurses or hospital. While in Khe Sanh he trained a selected few Bru and Vietnamese locals who had the capacity and interest in saving lives and he organized Vietnamese field sanitation teams. His job also was to help win the hearts and minds of the 800 families there by holding village Med Caps on a regular schedule. The transportation of local wounded and ill was a dicey undertaking as ill-equipped trucks bounced over terrain, so as part of the advisory team his job was to establish respectable medical care. Of course, intelligence was always part of the "bill of fare" and he was alert to the possibility of Viet Cong (VC) and sympathizers in the area.

He had taken it upon himself to contact a number of drug and food manufacturing companies in the United States and had been successful with a number of them. Pet Carnation sent thousands of pounds of Carnation Instant Breakfast mix to him both in Khe Sanh and the Bru/VN Khe Sanh refugee area in Cua Valley, the refugee resettlement area used for the Bru after their self-evacuation from Huong Hoa. He also received hundreds of pounds of badly needed soap. The soap was only partially successful because some of it smelled so good that the Bru ladies, unaccustomed to such a delightful commodity, refused to waste it on bathing. At another time in Cua Valley he was able to obtain a planeload of clothes for all the locals. Perhaps his greatest accomplishment was the numerous drug samples he was able to procure from American manufacturers, which went a long way in the treatment of various illnesses of the Bru. Another job of his was to establish a medical supply system for the locals. Supplies were difficult at best to procure but Doc Perry trained the people to get medical supplies on their own and to requisition supplies through the Vietnamese system.

Doc Perry remembers the hand to mouth existence that was the advisor's life at the end of a long and limited logistical supply line:

At the Khe Sanh Dispensary we had a makeshift examining table that many had lain on at one time or another. I periodically made scrounging missions to FOB-3 and the combat base. At one point I noticed a rather large crate was still sitting on the pierced steel planking (PSP) landing strip off ramp where it had sat for maybe a month. No markings were legible enough to read, all faded out. I approached an Air Force Sergeant standing near by. He coordinated outgoing shipments, in addition to other duties. I asked about the contents of this crate and lo and behold he said it was a rather new "clinic table" of some sort. I loosened a few boards and beheld a new operating room table!!! Apparently no one could determine who owned it or where it was destined. No paperwork! He was readying it for shipment to Danang, where is came from. "I can use it." He said that he couldn't tell me to just take it, but if it came up "missing," what could they do? I found two marines in Khe Sanh village driving a $^3/_4$ ton truck. They said that they'd help, so I grabbed 3 or 4 Bru and away we went to the airbase. We got it out of the crate and 'planted' it in the dispensary. It looked good in there! Really beautiful, a minor miracle. Then one sunny afternoon about 2 or 3 weeks later a Marine captain stopped by and approached me outside the dispensary. He said that they were looking for this crated operating room table that came up missing from the ramp at the airbase. They had found the rightful owner through a chain of events, he said. It seems that a Dr. Pat Smith had this out-patient clinic in Pleiku, that she was an OB/GYN specialist that had three months earlier, while in the States, coordinated the shipment of the table with a friend who turned out to be a US Senator. When it became lost she contacted the Senator. All hell broke loose, it seems. The Senator initiated inquiries, which landed in the lap of General Westmoreland's aide-de-camp. This set into motion a chain of events a mile long. This was 'high pressure' event stuff with the war on hold type setting. It seems someone, somehow came up with the invoice in Saigon and a major tracing began . . . all the way to the small Marine base in Khe Sanh. The Marine captain said: "if you have knowledge of its whereabouts somehow get it back to the air base and get all of the brass off our asses." I returned it that afternoon.

When it came down to the health issues of the 10,000 Bru and Vietnamese in Khe Sanh and later Cua Village, I became the caped crusader in that I did almost anything that I could to 'borrow' medical supplies. There was absolutely no other way!

John Roberts was the medical corpsman attached to the CAC-OSCAR Marines. John came from a family that had lived in Texas since before the Republic and had a proud heritage of military service by many members of his family. He attended Amarillo and Temple Junior Colleges and in 1966 enlisted in the U.S. Navy as a Hospital Corpsman and was assigned to CAP OSCAR.

John also remembers the hand-to-mouth existence of the CAP O-2 Marines.

On one such occasion, while I was distracting the docs at "Charlie-Med" (the Medical facility at the combat base) we were able to get a 5-gallon container of ethanol normally used in the pharmacy for cough medicine preparation or cleaning the radar scopes. It was the purest drinking alcohol you ever tasted. None of my Marines knew what it was and I kept it under my rack for several months (August to 24 December '67). Then I made a wonderful "jungle juice" for the lads. What a party time! I was glad there was a truce for Christmas '67. I remember that one of the Marines had a phonograph or tape player; anyway it got stuck on track saying, "because we are number one in the nation." We played it that way over and over for hours—what a hoot!

But in spite of the inaccessibility of the area, the lack of supplies, and the sometimes confusing or frustrating coordination between groups, the work of aiding and training the Bru continued. The major effort was improving the lot of the Bru.

In a letter home to his parents on August 17, LT Clarke wrote:

We had some mortar rounds come into a Special Forces camp about 4 kilometers away last night, which is the first evidence, except for bunkers, barbed wire and weapons, that I've seen of a war going on. We get reports of much enemy activity all around us (10 KM or more) but other than that things are quiet. Even with this, I still carry a weapon whenever I leave the compound because there's no reason to ask for trouble.

Yesterday I went with Major Whitenack, my boss, to the opening of a new Buddhist school. The school is right outside the wire of our compound as is the pagoda. We sat on a stage and nodded and clapped while different people made speeches and then we drank "café au lait." (I carried my pistol under my shirt so as to not embarrass anyone by bringing a weapon into the Pagoda.)

Monday afternoon we are going to open the new mid-wife house that has just been built by the local people using USAID (United States Agency for International Development) supplies and painted by the Marines. USAID also supplied the mid-wife kits. You might watch the papers as they are going to try and make a big publicity thing out of it. Things like this are better than the US funding a whole city for the Government of Vietnam for this the people designed and built themselves so they feel that it is theirs— not the US's. Also this mid-wife house is what they felt that the area needed most. We were lucky to get the supplies so that they could build it. This is not a high priority area, to be exact it is a low priority because of the small population and the distance from population centers. Everything we eat, drive, shoot and build with has to come in by air and when the weather is bad the planes can't fly.

From August through December of 1967, with minor exceptions, life was pretty rewarding and peaceful. Although hardly idyllic, the country was beautiful, wildlife was plentiful, monkeys in the trees with their ceaseless chatter, water buffalo everywhere, elephants, tigers, snakes of all kinds, invincible insects, and blood-sucking leeches. All of this plus jungle so dense that you could run and dive head first into the bush and still not penetrate more than a few inches. Navy Corpsman John Roberts, from CAC-OSCAR 2 remembers this time as:

> . . . monotonous and the real enemy was the jungle and mountainous terrain, coupled with a lack of sanitation. We seldom consciously thought about the NVA or the Viet Cong. Once in awhile, we would make enemy contact in an ambush, or observe enemy movements, but for months we busied ourselves holding Med Caps for the three local villages.
>
> The Marines were assigned the mission of providing security for the villages against the Viet Cong and NVA. As a CAC the Marines had a two-fold task. We were told that we were in a war for the hearts and minds of the Vietnamese peoples. We accepted that mission with a certain degree of enthusiasm. The Marines worked well with the local villagers and particularly well with the Montagnard tribesmen. At OSCAR 2, we had far more association with the Bru than we did with the Vietnamese. We all shared a common respect for the Bru. We felt that they were more trustworthy than the Vietnamese, and that they were certainly more deserving of any security and support we could afford them.
>
> The Bru were very interesting for me personally. I tried to learn as much about them as I could. Our Platoon Sergeant, Roy Harper, had seen more time in country that anyone else I knew about and he briefed me on the cultural aspects as much as he could. We learned much more from SGT Dan Kelly, who was the only Marine who could speak their language fluently. SGT Kelly, a man we all greatly respected, used his considerable influence

with the company commander and ultimately the Base Commander to give relief to the Bru whenever possible.

Local Churchmen, a Catholic priest, and two missionaries, John and Carolyn Miller, and their children also intervened on behalf of the Bru on many occasions. The necessity for intervention was sometimes thought to be racial, in that the Vietnamese considered them as primitives, void of educational skills and personal merit.

My own feeling was then and is now that they, like the American Indian, were viciously maligned by political operatives who really did not know the Bru and wanted only to be rid of the problem. Their diversity, dignity and courage were never recognized by the Vietnamese or US high commands. They were later to suffer horrendous casualties during the Siege of Khe Sanh.

On September 24, 1967, LT Clarke wrote his parents:

Time continues to pass. Today marks the end of my 2nd month in country. Everyday I learn something or see something new. Yesterday I went on a wood cutting detail with about 30 local soldiers. I found a coffee plantation that I didn't even know existed and met the French owner, Llinares. This Frenchman lives a hermitic existence. He lives in a large stone building, which serves as his home and warehouse. He seems to live on rice and the grapefruit (local version) and bananas that grow wild throughout the area.

The reason that we were cutting wood was that we had to build tin roofs over the bunkers before they collapse. We'd had 5 straight days of continuous pouring rain and mud in sandbags gets a lot heavier when it is wet. Bunkers can collapse from this. The Marines at the base had one collapse, which injured 11 people and killed one. If the rains don't come back for about 3 more days we'll have tin roofs over all of our bunkers.

There were incessant rumors that Felix Poillane—the other French coffee grower—was providing support for the NVA while being friendly to the Americans. This report was never substantiated but persisted. He was constantly seeking to find ways to export his coffee. He was later killed in the crash of a U.S. cargo plane returning to Khe Sanh.

CPT Nhi explains how he was able to overcome the animosity of the societal elements and build a team.

In my opinion, morale building always starts with trust. I needed the trust of the Bru and the Vietnamese. I did many right things to earn the trust of the Bru. One highlight was that after 3 months on the job, no matter where I went, Bru PFs were my only security people. Besides a Vietnamese radioman, I entrusted my safety to Hom and his men. The Bru watched enthusiastically the scene in which the district chief was surrounded by only

Bru PFs. To the simple mind of the Bru, if I could trust them this much, they certainly could do the same to me in return. It was more difficult to earn the Vietnamese trust. However, I did make it happen. Being a Dalat graduate carried a lot of weight with the Vietnamese soldiers. RF companies spent their 6 months tour in one district after another. They knew all of the district chiefs very well. I was somewhat different from the rest. I earned the respect of cadres and, civilians in my area of responsibility. The province chief and his staff had never bothered me in any way.

On October 15, 1968, LT Clarke followed up the above letter to his parents with the following:

Today is Sunday so we're not really working. Unless there is something big going on the Vietnamese don't work on Saturday afternoon and Sunday. This morning I went to one of the villages with SGT Perry, our medic, and he treated about 55 people, mostly for skin diseases and infections. He treats at least that many people a day in a different village each day of the week and then next week he starts over again.

For the last couple of days I've been going around the area with 2 people from the coast. They are here, at my urging, to check on the feasibility of building a brick factory in this area. This is a set of manual machines where you mix 1 part cement with 9 parts clay, put it under pressure and ZAP—a brick. If we can get this in operation we'll be able to build latrines, schools, bathhouses, and many other things besides the Bru being able to sell the bricks so that they'll have money to buy food and clothes. If I can get this machinery here along with the needed cement, I'll be able to build a lot and it will be quite a feather in my cap. I am going to write a plan for the whole thing … The potential with this is just out of this world and these people need so much.

Both CPT Nhi and CPT Clarke were promoted on November 1, 1967. They celebrated their promotion to captain with a party at "Howard Johnson's." CPT Nhi was responsible for providing the food and CPT Clarke provided the beverages. One of the more popular drinks was 10 High Bourbon, which could be purchased for about $2.50 a bottle. Several Marines from CAC "O," Special Forces personnel from Lang Vei and FOB-3, local Vietnamese and Bru officials and some special guests attended the party from Laos. The 33rd Royal Laotian Battalion was just across the border and was in constant coordination with the Special Forces from Lang Vei and FOB-3. The battalion commander and several of his officers happened to be in the area on a coordination meeting and were obviously welcome guests.

The province advisor now had a new deputy, LTC Joe Seymoe. Seymoe was a straight arrow, spit and polish, a soldier that lived by the book.

Brewer didn't care for him much. On November 4, 1967, CPT Clarke wrote his parents:

> We've gotten a new Colonel and he is a strong believer in Regulations and spit and polish. Also if you can't get the Vietnamese to do something then you are to do it yourself. This really defeats the whole purpose of our being here for if they know that we'll do the work for them they'll just sit by and watch. The Bru are not this way at all, they'll try to do what you suggest, though you usually have to show them how. If we're working on something the Bru will come over and help us. The Vietnamese treat the Bru like savages and as simple laborers while the Americans treat them as equals and this has won a lot of friends. Needless to say I think the world of the Bru.

On November 23, the new captain wrote to his parents:

> The promotion to Captain also means that when Major Whitenack, my present boss, goes home in a week, I'll take over as the District Advisor, which is pretty good for a junior Captain. They don't expect a replacement for the major until next May, so it should be a good experience.
>
> Today was Thanksgiving. They were supposed to fly turkey and all the trimmings out to us, but the weather closed in so we ate the cold marine leftovers. Oh well, today wasn't much different from any other day …
>
> Things have been pretty quiet except for a few shots and a few mortar rounds. The small arms fire has been a total of five rounds in two months and the mortar rounds all landed 300 meters from the compound. Charlie just seems to leave us alone, which doesn't bother me at all. The District Chief doesn't like to go out very often as if we hit anything it very possibly could be an NVA Battalion so we continue to march in other areas. Civic Action is one of my big areas.

In late November 1967, MAJ Whitenack and SFC Humphries left and things began to change. The five-man advisory team, headed by CPT Clarke now included SFCs King, Perry, and Kasper and Specialist Four Gehrke. COL David Lounds commanded the Khe Sanh Combat Base. MAJ Duncan was in charge of FOB-3. CPT Frank Willoughby commanded Special Forces Detachment A-101 in the new Lang Vei Special Forces Camp. LT Tom Stamper commanded CAC-OSCAR.

Of all the men at Khe Sanh village LT Stamper had the most previous amount of combat experienced from earlier assignments. Prior to January 1968, his duty station was at Con Thien where he commanded an infantry company. Con Thien was one of several outposts along the DMZ which had the mission of limiting North Vietnamese infiltration thru the DMZ. Because of the proximity of these outposts to North Vietnam they were shelled frequently and there were major battles to stem the infiltration. These were some of the bloodiest fights that the Marines were involved in all of Vietnam. Con Thien sustained the worst losses of all Marine bases during the entire Vietnam War. LT Stamper's company was caught in the largest enemy barrage of the Con Thien artillery battle. The losses were substantiality more than 50 percent and were attributed to months of enemy artillery fire, which was second only to the Siege of Khe Sanh in Marine history of the Vietnam War.

These losses and months of enduring incoming NVA artillery fire left this lieutenant depressed and weary of being in command. He had volunteered for the Combined Action Program (CAP). The CAP unit at Khe Sanh village had not endured any combat since May 1967; it was a great place for Tom to strengthen his shattered nerves, not knowing that he was about to be involved in the largest and longest artillery siege of the war—the 77-day siege of the Khe Sanh Combat Base (KSCB).

CPT Clarke brought a different perspective to the advisory mission. He perceived himself as a facilitator, expediter, and helper. He sought to avoid confrontations with the district chief. He did not go to the Combat Base to inspect the local inhabitants that were getting off aircraft. He also was not willing to go head to head with LT Stamper to clean up responsibilities. He did, however, insure that Stamper knew who the senior U.S. officer on the scene was.

Chapter 5

GIAP'S STRATEGY

Meanwhile, back in Hanoi...

Despite the controversy over whether the Tet Offensive and the siege on Khe Sanh was anticipated or not, undertaking such an effort indicated that the NVA, in spite of heavy losses, still had enormous strength and lasting power. They were determined to take back their country.

The Vietnamese nation had been waging war against enemies for centuries and the brilliant and innovative military strategist Tran Hung Dao looms large in their military history. Tran Hung Dao was named commander of Vietnam's armed forces as the Mongols, under the great general Kublai Khan, looked to expand their empire from China in the early 1280s. Tran adopted a defensive position when the Mongols moved into northern Vietnam in 1283, then employed guerrilla warfare and scorched-earth tactics to set up a counteroffensive that drove the Mongols back into China. Tran Hung Dao's legacy of guerrilla warfare against a more powerful enemy was a model for twentieth-century Communist guerrillas. His legacy to his country, a call for national unity and resistance, inspired the North Vietnamese during the Indochina wars of 1946–1975.

In Tran Hung Dao's book, *Summary of Military Strategy*, we find the basic Vietnamese approach:

> When the enemy is away from home for a long time and produces no victories, and families learn of their dead, then the enemy population becomes dissatisfied. Time is always in our favor. Our climate, mountains, and jungles discourage the enemy.

GEN Vo Nguyen Giap, commander of the NVA during the Vietnam War, was strongly influenced by Dao's strategic thought. He also had the determined support of the North Vietnamese people.

GEN Giap created the concept of the Tet Offensive. It was Giap who had masterminded the long, arduous campaign of the Viet Minh against the French forces in Indochina. It was he who had guided his forces to victory in the well-known battle of Dien Bien Phu. It was this battle that broke the back of French political resolve and eventually led to the division of the country. Giap understood that the "victory had been won on the streets of Paris," as a result of the press reports surrounding the siege and eventual fall of Dien Bien Phu. The French political will had been undermined by the continual press stories of what Bernard Fall, a French author of several works about the Indochina War, was to call "Hell in a Very Small Place."

It was during the summer of 1967, after evaluating the situation in South Vietnam and aware of the increasing losses his forces were suffering, that Giap began making plans for an all-out attack. It was not a reckless, hot-headed move, but a calculated risk—one that included testing U.S. intentions.

Giap was fearful of a U.S. attack north of the DMZ. He saw Khe Sanh as being an important base in support of such an attack. To test U.S. intentions he conducted operations and attacks east of Khe Sanh against Con Thien and Cam Lo in the spring and summer of 1967 to determine whether the United States would react and counterattack and invade the North. When the United States failed to react, Giap felt free to relocate his forces from the defense of the DMZ and to conduct his planned attack. To facilitate this plan he created a new Front Headquarters to control forces along and south of the DMZ. U.S. radio intercept analysts monitored the creation of this new front. In October of 1967 intelligence indicated that there was a threat against Khe Sanh.

Giap understood Western thinking—everything in the West had to be done in a hurry. Conversely, the Vietnamese were in no hurry. They had been at war with one country or another for hundreds of years. The Vietnamese tactical doctrine can be described as "the four fasts and one slow." This meant fast advance, fast assault, fast clearance of the battlefield, and fast withdrawal—all based on slow preparation.

To demonstrate to the world that the Communist forces were "alive and well," a general toe-to-toe attack against the Americans would clearly demonstrate their determination not to give up. It would target the political consensus in the United States. It would demonstrate the political strength to continue against great odds. It would prove that the Vietnamese resolve was stronger than that of the United States.

Giap knew it would be costly, but the political advantages far outweighed the military disadvantages of large casualties. This same type of Pyrrhic victory at Dien Bien Phu in 1954 had brought about the defeat and departure of the French. There was no reason to believe that this would not be the case with a similar triumph against the United States. Giap believed that if his forces enjoyed even partial success, the will to fight might be taken away from the American people.

Giap's strategy was simple. For the last 3 years, the bulk of the fighting had occurred in the remote provinces of South Vietnam. The major cities, apart from occasional terrorist attacks, had been largely left alone. The Tet offensive would be initiated with a concentration of two North Vietnamese divisions against the American stronghold at Khe Sanh in the northwestern mountains of South Vietnam.

Once Allied attention was diverted to Khe Sanh, attacks would occur in dozens of towns and cities, including Saigon. These attacks would create chaos and political unrest. The urban areas were defended almost exclusively by South Vietnamese troops as the U.S. troops were in the rural areas seeking out the main line NVA and VC units. Giap calculated that over 50 percent of Army of Vietnam (ARVN) forces would be out celebrating the Lunar New Year—Tet. It was hoped that these surprise rapid blows could even possibly incite the populace of South Vietnam to rise against the "puppet" government and against the United States; perhaps even cause an overthrow of the government. At a minimum, the psychological impact of the ferocity of the attacks would be convincing to the American people and the politicians in Washington that there was not a "light at the end of the tunnel." Giap was willing to bring the VC infrastructure out into the open in this endeavor. This created the risk that the VC would be decimated in the Tet Offensive. He was willing to sacrifice the VC in support of the larger goal of turning American public opinion against the war.

If only one major city could be taken and held, a provisional Communist government set up and the National Liberation Front seen as being in control, then the effort would have been successful. Although any large metropolis would do, Saigon and Hue were considered the top priorities. The reason for trying to take and control Saigon was self-evident—it was the nation's capital and most populated city. Hue, the "Ancient City," was quite valuable for its historical importance to the Vietnamese. It could possibly be the Communist's "Coup de Grace." Even should this effort fail, it was understood that the entire effort would politically turn the American people once and for all against the war. With pressure from the population, U.S. leaders would have no choice but to bring an end to American participation in the war. With American manpower and firepower removed, the taking of South Vietnam would be a simple thing. This was the strategic thinking and motivation behind the North Vietnamese attacks on Khe Sanh and the Tet Offensive of January 1968. The military, political and psychological aspects were well blended. The strategic acumen demonstrated by this blending should be learned by all future strategists. Giap's vision of the outcome was prophetic in its accuracy.

The beginning of the execution of the Communist plan, officially known as "Tong Cong Kich–Tong Khoi Nghia, (TCK-TKN)" or "General Offensive/General Uprising," began in the fall of 1967. It was at that time that U.S. intelligence sources detected a buildup of enemy forces near Khe Sanh. There was strong evidence of the presence of two full enemy divisions, the 304th and the 325C, with various other units in the area. The units from the hill fights of the spring had learned many lessons and planned to exploit the lessons learned.

As noted earlier, the Khe Sanh plateau had been the center of numerous previous firefights as U.S. Marines took control of the hills controlling the plateau from the Communists. It was a vital point in controlling the influx of North Vietnamese that had come south along the Ho Chi Minh Trail through Laos.

Giap saw in the battle for Khe Sanh many parallels to a siege he had led 14 years earlier against the French in Dien Bien Phu. He had, however, no grand illusions about the same sort of victory there. The conditions were different and the cards definitely stacked against the Communists. Still, anything was possible, and he did not discount a remote chance that the campaign to capture Khe Sanh would be victorious. The trump card for the Communists would come only weeks later with the Tet Offensive. The two complemented each other perfectly. Either could be successful and result in the desired political victory. Both could fail and still result in a political victory, by convincing the American people of the limited utility of continuing the war.

There is debate as to whether Khe Sanh was an attempt to get the United States to divert troops away from the defense of the cities and thus increase the probability of success for the Tet attacks or an effort to repeat Dien Bien Phu. In actuality, it was both. Khe Sanh attracted all of the attention while the final preparations were made for the Tet Offensive. Conversely, the Tet Offensive pulled away forces that could have reinforced Lang Vei or allowed for the reestablishment of the District Headquarters. In essence the two were complementary.

THE NVA TACTICAL PLAN

The plan for the initial attacks on Khe Sanh divided the area into two sectors. The northern sector belonged to the 325C Division. This included the area north of the Combat Base and the hills. The area to the south of the Combat Base was the responsibility of the 304th Division.

On December 6, 1967, the Central Party Military Committee established the Command Headquarters and Party Committee for the Highway 9–Khe Sanh Campaign. The command post for the campaign headquarters was established at Sap Lit, located near the borders of North and South Vietnam and Laos in the southwestern end of the DMZ.

The objectives of the opening attacks of the campaign were varied. Elements of the NVA 325th Division were to attack Hill 861. Elements of the 304th Division were to attack Huong Hoa Subsector (aka Khe Sanh village), on Highway 9, during the night of January 20, 1968, and draw American and Republic of Vietnam Armed Forces relief forces from the Marine bases along the DMZ at the Rockpile and Ca Lu and attack them.

On January 9, 1968, the NVA campaign headquarters assigned responsibility for the area south of the Khe Sanh Combat Base, including the Huong Hoa Subsector, to the 304th Infantry Division. The command post for the 304th Division was established near Lang Troai on the border of Vietnam and Laos south of Lang Vei.

According to NVA reports, beginning January 21, the 7th Battalion, 66th Regiment, 304th Division, supported by unspecified artillery units (probably drawn from the 675th or 45th Artillery Regiments) was to attack and occupy Huong Hoa subsector. Prior to the 7th Battalion's attack on Huong Hoa subsector, the 9th Regiment, 304th Division, was to send one platoon to occupy the Ku Boc road junction—the junction of the road to Combat Base and Route 9. Another platoon was to occupy the high ground in the vicinity of Hill 471. They were to hold these two features at all costs. The 9th Battalion of the 66th Regiment was to occupy positions close to Highway 9.

THE AMERICAN PLAN

In Washington, Defense Intelligence Agency (DIA) analysts were predicting an attack on Khe Sanh. Their predictions were not accepted by the policymakers because of the contradiction with the political "reality" that the war was being won. Of course, it was this same set of analysts who either failed to predict the Tet '68 Offensive that occurred 10 days later or whose intelligence estimates and forecasted NVA actions were ignored. It is interesting that they knew months in advance that the effort against Khe Sanh was coming, but there allegedly was no knowledge about the Tet Offensive. There is a growing school of thought to suggest that some in the

Saigon-based U.S. leadership knew that something around Tet was coming, but did not want to tip their hands that they knew.

As for Khe Sanh, intelligence sources had detected the movement of significant forces into the area and GEN Westmoreland had decided in early January to fight a major fight in the Khe Sanh area. (Was this part of a massive NVA deception plan in preparation for Tet '68 some wonder?) Westmoreland's decision to hold the Combat Base was based on his desire to conduct ground operations into Laos at a later date.

This is substantiated by the following January 21, 1968, GEN Westmoreland, COMUSMACV, Saigon, message to GEN Wheeler, chairman of the Joint Chiefs of Staff, Washington:

1. The anticipated enemy attack on Khe Sanh was initiated last evening. Khe Sanh military installation has been under constant rocket and mortar fire since early morning, and Hill 861 has been under ground attack. Ammunition and POL dumps have been hit, with fire and explosions reported by Air Force Forward Air Controllers (FAC). 7AF is maintaining an airborne command post and FACs (Forward Air Controllers) in the area. There is an NVA build-up north of the DMZ and in Base Areas 101 west of Quang Tri and 114 west of Hue. The next several weeks are destined to be active.

2. The following actions have been taken:

   a. On 6 Jan a coordinated intelligence collection effort was initiated on the Khe Sanh area (Niagara I) using maximum available resources.

   b. On 6 Jan, I directed Gen Momyer (the air component commander of US forces in Vietnam) to prepare a plan to concentrate all available air resources into the Khe Sanh area (Niagara II).

   c. On 17 Jan the 1st Air Cavalry Division minus one Brigade began to deploy to Hue/Phu Bai, and will close tomorrow.

   d. On 18 Jan two additional Vietnamese Airborne Battalions deployed to Hue, making a total of four in the area.

   e. On the 19th, I diverted all B-52 strikes to the area.

   f. Based on my visit to III MAF on 19 January, I sent my J2 to Khe Sanh on 20 January to insure coordination of reconnaissance activities in and around Khe Sanh.

   g. On the 19th, I directed Gen Cushman (I Corps and III MAF Commander) to deploy the 3D Brigade of the 1st Air Cavalry Division as soon as practical from the Wheeler-Wallowa area to Hue/Phu Bai to join its parent division.

   h. On 20 January, I instructed LTG Weyand (II Corps Commander) to deploy the 2D Brigade of the 101st Airborne Division to Hue/Phu Bai for attachment to 1st Cavalry Division as soon as airlift becomes available, probably about 23 January.

i. Based on plans initiated last week, I directed Gen Momyer on 20 January to divert any useful "dump truck" assets [a combination of anti personnel mines and sensors that were being deployed into Laos] from the Muscle Shoals Project to the Quang Tri area.

j. On 20 January, I instructed LTG Cushman to defer any further work on the trace involved in the dye marker project [dye marker was a project to build defensive positions along the DMZ, which would link with "dump truck" to limit infiltration into South Vietnam] so as to keep maximum troops available to react to enemy initiatives.

k. Today, I am sending Gen Abrams to III MAF (General Westmoreland's Deputy and successor) to assess the situation. Also I have directed Gen Momyer to station a liaison officer at Khe Sanh.

This message shows actions long before the initial attack and highlights that GEN Westmoreland knew that the attack against Khe Sanh was coming, he wanted to have it, and made no efforts to advise the people outside of the Combat Base of his intentions. His goal was to fight a set-piece, firepower-intensive, attrition fight in which the NVA would sustain significant losses. It is also important to note all of the resources that were being moved to the area of Hue. If Khe Sanh was a deception operation and Hue was one of the critical objectives for the Tet Offensive, then the deception was working against the possible NVA objective of securing Hue. However, despite the reinforcements earmarked for Hue, in actuality, most of Hue was seized by the NVA, though part of the citadel and the MACV compound never did fall.

On the Marine Corps Birthday, November 10, 1967, COL Lounds addressed the 26th Marines on Hill 881 with these ominous words, "You all will soon be in the American history books."

Other steps that were being taken to prepare for the battle have come to light from recently unclassified documents:

• On December 13, 1967, reinforcement of Khe Sanh began with the arrival of 3/26 Marines. The documents state that "Reinforcement could not progress too quickly lest the NVA be aware we knew their intentions." Accordingly, 2/26 didn't arrive until January 17. The 2nd and 3rd battalions had joined the 1st which had been the only battalion at Khe Sanh before then. At this point the entire 26th Marine Regiment was together for the first time since coming ashore.

• In the meantime, knowing Khe Sanh would be hit, the first phase of Operation NIAGARA was launched on January 5, 1968. (Operation NIAGARA was to be a saturation bombing campaign by B-52s of the area around Khe Sanh and was set to commence, interestingly, on January 21, and Phase I, beginning January 5, was for target-selection.) The operation was approved by the American Ambassador to Laos (Sullivan) on January 16 and by CINCPAC on January 17.

- On January 10, the CIA concluded Khe Sanh was to be the target of a major NVA attack.
- On January 12, General Westmoreland requested JCS declassify COFRAM munitions (Controlled Fragmentation, also known as "Firecracker") for use in nonpopulated areas of I Corps (that is, Khe Sanh). On January 13, a portion of the ammunition dump at Khe Sanh was relocated.
- On January 14, III MAF was directed to review the plans for support of Lang Vei should it be attacked.

Chapter 6

THE SITUATION CHANGES—THE PRELUDE TO THE BATTLE IN KHE SANH

The time between August and December of 1967 was a time of relative peace in the Khe Sanh village compound. A good deal of progress was being made in the aid and training of the Bru and the military personnel were enjoying a somewhat quiet time with only infrequent interruptions by sporadic gunfire. But in December of 1967 the situation started to change. The Marines at the Combat Base started to improve their fighting positions, resupply efforts increased, and the airfield repair effort intensified. At the end of the month a 2/26 Marines arrived bringing to two the number of battalions at the Combat Base.

The advisory team visited the Combat Base every day for water resupply. The water in the village contained parasites that made the water undrinkable to Westerners. The Marines operated a water point and pumped the water several kilometers from the river to the inside of the perimeter of the Combat Base where it was treated. The daily enemy situation reports that the advisory team picked up when they refilled their water cans showed no significant changes in the enemy situation. What was going on, CPT Clarke began asking himself with ever increasing urgency.

The advisory team, the Lang Vei Special Forces and SOG were constantly seeking to find out why all of the activity was occurring. No one at the Combat Base would tell them. This was just one more instance of the bad blood that existed between the Marine leadership at the Combat Base and Army elements throughout the area.

Prados and Stubbe, in their work, *Valley of Decision: The Siege of Khe Sanh*, write:

> The Marines tended to view the Green Berets as an undisciplined rabble, while the Special Forces saw the jar heads as a collection of clumsy, over-armed, over-heavy units who would never be able to cope with the VC and NVA.

This characterization is accurate and portrays not only the Marine–Special Forces relationship, but also the Army–Marine Corps relationship. A standard joke among soldiers at Khe Sanh was that the Marines judged their success by how uncomfortable they were—the more misery, the more success. (For example, the CAP O-1 Marines went to the local parasite-infested stream and bathed in the fast current while the advisory team fashioned a shower out of two welded together 55 gallon drums, some pipe, a shower head and an emersion heater. The Marines of O-2 had a similar shower and they, too, were able to get a hot shower every night.) The soldiers at the Lang Vei Camp, the advisory team, and FOB-3 established their own radio codes and frequencies to insure confidential communications, because the Marines were listening in on the prescribed frequencies. In short the soldiers didn't trust the Marines. This is a theme that runs throughout the history of Khe Sanh.

Province Headquarters was faring no better. It didn't have any information to provide other than to join in the guessing as to why the Marines were making all of the preparations that they were. Bob Brewer, province senior advisor, visited the District Headquarters around the end of the year. CPT Clarke advised him of his uncertainty as to what the Marines were preparing to deal with. He told Clarke he would try to reinforce him, if the time came, by way of the coffee plantation just south of the perimeter. The trees there were only 6 or 7-feet tall and he felt they could easily be leveled in advance by fighter-bombers so that a heliborne air assault could land. CPT Clarke found it very doubtful that Brewer, a CIA man, did not know what was going on.

Christmas came and went with little activity, except an unsuccessful probe against the joint radio relay site on Hill 950 (across the river from the Combat Base). From this hill one could see the entire Khe Sanh plateau. This relay site was going to be critical less than a month later. The advisory team and Marines of CAC O joined with the local Christian community for a candle-lit service at the local church.

CPT Clarke wrote his parents on December 26, 1967:

> Well, Christmas has gone past us for another year. We had a 24-hour truce, which was only marked by one VC violation here, but I've heard that there were over 100 in the country. Here they mortared and attacked a Marine

radio relay site, wounding five Marines. We went to the local church for a midnight service. It was funny to see all of the weapons stacked at the door. I carried my pistol under my uniform.

On January 10, COL Lounds told his staff to expect a major attack in 10 days and then on January 15, he required his troops to wear flak jackets and helmets at all times. This information was never passed on to any of the Army elements in the area although recently unclassified documents state that:

The senior Marine Generals, knowing by November, 1967 that the NVA were about to wage a major offensive around the end of January, 1968, had assumed Camp Carroll (to the east of Khe Sanh along the DMZ) to be the target. At a gathering of Generals and intelligence staffs and technicians, the technicians from Signals Intelligence (SIGINT) convinced the Generals that the main target would be Khe Sanh.

The Marines never shared their knowledge, but the activity did prompt the District Advisory Team to suggest to the district chief that the defenses should be improved. Several bunkers were reinforced and strengthened. Efforts were made to clear the fields of fire, as they were limited in numerous places. Several new barbed-wire obstacles and new bunker locations were placed. One of these bunkers was placed on top of the AID warehouse on the southeastern part of the compound. From there the PFs controlled a critical avenue of approach and could prevent the NVA from hiding behind the warehouse. CPT Nhi explains how this critical bunker got built:

I instructed Hom to select 3 of the most trustworthy PFs among his men. This group of three would be given a special mission. Immediately they set about filling as many sand bags as they could in a hurry. After the front gate was closed and the surrounding area was getting dark, Hom and the 3 men moved the filled sand bags to the top of the warehouse. They constructed a bunker that was barely large enough for 3 persons. For camouflage purposes, the bunker was covered with tree branches before dawn and the whole day. The 3 PFs took their positions in the bunker after dark. Their mission was to use hand grenades only to eliminate any enemies who used the warehouse as cover to approach the defensive perimeter. The success of this team depended on keeping their positions hidden and unknown to the enemy as long as possible. Therefore they we not allowed to use their rifles during the hours of darkness. They could use them only for self defense.

Patrols were increased and a new backup communications plan was worked out and the advisory team, for the first time, had a reasonable chance of getting a message out of Khe Sanh and eventually to some one who could provide help. The primary route was through a Special Forces' radio relay team on top of Hill 950, across the valley and on top of one of the highest mountains in the area.

The CAC units made emergency preparations in reaction to the Marine activity. They assumed that the advisory team had some information and they followed the lead. John Roberts recounts the improvements made at CAP OSCAR 2 on the western edge of the village in reaction to the lack of information:

> In disgust, we returned to our compound and began to lay in all the supplies and ammunition we could requisition, beg, borrow, or steal.
>
> We set up a virtual barrier of claymore mines in every direction facing outwards from our perimeter. We began double-checking the radio call signs and coding sheets to insure our ability to communicate with the base fire support center. We dug out our trenches a foot deeper, cleaned our fighting bunkers, and reinforced the weak points along all fighting positions. Cases of hand grenades were strategically placed in between each fighting position. Precious medical supplies were stockpiled and placed in protected areas. Flak jackets, helmets, and gas masks were strategically positioned near fighting holes. Finally, additional tanglefoot and concertina wire were laid in every avenue of approach to the defensive compound. On January 19th, 1968 OSCAR 2 was ready! We would soon need it all, and more!

The District Chief had been busily engaged in preparations for several years. CPT Nhi recounts:

> The battle of Khe Sanh Village lasted only 24 hours yet the preparation for the defense of the District Headquarters had been ongoing since June 1966, the month I took over Huong Hoa District as its chief. My attention at the time was focused on the physical condition of the bunkers. All of the bunkers and walls were built with logs and they were old and getting rotten. I had no choice but to rebuild them. Getting materials for the job posed a big challenge. I couldn't count on Quang Tri's support for the project. Fortunately, Navy SeaBees were building a new airstrip for the future Marine Combat Base. I contacted a SeaBee officer at the scene asking him to let my RFs and PFs pick up few hundred pieces of PSP (pierced steel planning) that were in good condition. We rebuilt the bunkers one after another and repaired the walls one section at a time. It took us about 4 months to complete the job.

Simultaneous with the improvements to the District Headquarters' defenses improvements were happening at Lang Vei as well. The new camp was finished and occupied. It was a show place of the type of camp that Defense

Secretary McNamara wanted established throughout the border regions as part of the effort to limit infiltration into Vietnam.

The Americans in the Khe Sanh compound assumed a higher level of alert. The tension and anticipation were evident in nerves stretched taunt. One night the advisory team Watch NCO was chasing a rat with a broom. When he entered the sleeping quarters all one could hear was the cocking of four .45 pistols. "Hold it, it's me" came the frantic cry. There was the sound of magazines dropping out of pistols, rounds being ejected and reloaded in their magazines. Not another word was spoken. The next morning there was some discussion as to how lightly everyone was sleeping.

The secrecy reached the level of absurd the afternoon before the fight began. CPT Clarke and his small team were out on a sweep operation with the district chief and the RF Company in an area about 8 kilometers southwest of the District Headquarters when they received a radio call. The Special Forces at Lang Vei called to say that the operation had to be terminated and that the small force had to be clear of the area within 60 minutes. Further discussion revealed that this message had come from the Marines, but that they had lost contact with the District Headquarters and had thus called Lang Vei hoping that it could get the word out. Without any real reasons and in spite of wanting to finish the sweep, CPT Nhi called his forces in and they quickly left the area. Ninety minutes later a B-52 ARC light-strike went into the area that the small District Force had been searching. An ARC Light is a B-52 strike. Three bombers in formation drop bombs resulting in a saturation bombing of an area approximately 1 kilometer wide and 3 kilometers long.

The advisory team later learned that 3rd Battalion of the 26th Marines had been in a major fight between Hills 881 North and South that same day. That was the same day an NVA soldier, LT Tonc, surrendered just outside the wire of the Combat Base. He freely provided detailed information about the enemy's dispositions and plan of attack for Khe Sanh. That information was sent by courier to 3rd Marine Headquarters, though none of it was shared with the advisors or Special Forces personnel. Tonc claimed that the Khe Sanh campaign was being controlled directly by the North Vietnamese Defense Ministry and that its goal was to seize Quang Tri province by attacking from west to east. None of this information made it to the advisory team.

Unbeknownst to the small band of Army advisors, Marines, Vietnamese, and Bru warriors, the scene was set for the largest ground battle of the siege of Khe Sanh. The peacefulness that had been the Khe Sanh plateau was about to change and with it the careers and lives of over 6,000 men. CPT Clarke enjoyed his hot shower that evening, not knowing that it was the last peaceful shower that he was going to get for months.

Chapter 7

THE BATTLE IS JOINED

The NVA began its attack at 5 AM on January 21 with a ground assault on Hill 861, followed by rocket artillery and mortar fire on the Combat Base. As a result of a direct hit to one of the Ammo Storage Points, 1,500 tons of ammunition exploded, throwing fragments and unexploded rounds into the air in a conflagration of heat and noise that resounded throughout the Khe Sanh district. The fire ate the ammunition dump with a rapaciousness that would be stamped in the memory of those Marines that fled from the intensity of that eruption. Reaching beyond the boundaries of the Huong Hoa district, photos of the explosions were published in American newspapers and shook the public's complacency about the war. The significance of the loss of this ammunition was greater still to the isolated defenders in the village of Khe Sanh because now the Combat Base's ability to support them with artillery would be impacted.

The attack on the Combat Base awoke the advisory team and the Marines in the District Compound at the village. The advisors and Marines both immediately called a general alert and brought all of the Vietnamese and Montagnard occupants to a full state of readiness. As it turned out, the District Headquarters had about 30 minutes to prepare for an attack on the compound. Because of the fog the NVA had difficulty getting into position, giving the village needed time.

SFC Jim Perry, the advisory team medic, remembers that morning:

All four of the Advisory Team members were sleeping lightly when we were awakened by distant explosions. SFCs Kasper and King, along with myself, made it to our bunker in front of the District Headquarters building. We could hear numerous rounds striking the bunker's sandbags surrounding the three of us. The NVA knew exactly where we were. Each of the four advisory team members had a price on his head. CPT Clarke made it quickly back to the command bunker. The three of us in the front emptied several magazines, firing toward the pagoda on the west side of the compound. I carried a Thompson sub-machine gun and wore a 45 automatic. These accompanied me everywhere I went—to the villes [slang for villages] for Med Caps, in my bunk with me every night, even to the toilet.

George Amos, in a letter home to his wife, described the start of the battle.

I am not sure how to begin this letter because I am so glad to able to be writing it to you tonite. Don't worry, I am fine *Thank God*. But, I've been in one hell of a fight. I'll describe the events that happened. On Sunday morning about 4 AM [actually 5 AM] our compound started receiving incoming 82 mm mortar rounds. We slept thru them until about 4:45. Then Jim (Taronji), my tentmate, got up to see what was happening. He came running back to the tent and said "Get to the bunker, we're under attack." I hopped out of bed and ran to the cement bunker which had been assigned to us. (I later found an unexploded mortar round less than a foot from my tent. (God Loves Me!) At exactly 5 AM the NVA attacked. We fired everything we had at them and they still kept coming.

A human enemy is not always the greatest foe. Quite often nature itself is the greater obstacle to victory, and on the morning of January 21, 1968, a rich fog had slipped down from the mountains, settling like a heavy curtain on the District Compound. A weapon more deadly than guns, the fog became a predator, obscuring clarity, causing delays and irritation, and throwing warriors into a fearful position of feeling alone in the impenetrable blanket. Each man would be fighting by himself, unable to see from one fighting position to the next. He would be fighting independently based on what he could see within a very tight circle around himself.

The real advantage the NVA had was being able to come close without being observed because of the fog and the terrain, trees, and the pagoda. The treachery of the fog allowed them get within 15 meters of the compound's surrounding moat filled with punji stakes. The pagoda provided great cover and concealment, enabling the enemy to get very close without exposing themselves and created a seam between the French fort to the rear and the main compound.

George Amos describes the early morning as a "time that dense fog hung over the area." When it "lifted air support was called in, as were helicopters with supplies and *ammo*. We were very low on ammo. When the planes arrived they were immediately met by antiaircraft fire and the first US plane to make a bombing run was promptly shot down. Helicopters with reinforcements and ammo tried all day to get to us but were unable to do so. (1 helicopter lost)."

The defenders were attacked on three fronts within the confines of the village and at the CAP OSCAR 2 outpost several hundred meters to the west. The first front was the French Fort, manned by the Regional Force Company of about 60 Vietnamese soldiers commanded by a Vietnamese lieutenant who was killed in the battle. The second front was the main compound defended by the OSCAR 1 Marines and CAC Headquarters Marines, LT Tom Stamper, and Gunnery Sergeant Boyda. SGT John Balanco was the Marine on the ground commanding CAP OSCAR 1. In addition, there were 50 Popular Force Bru soldiers, CPT Nhi and his staff of about ten. The advisory team of four made up the rest. The third front was CAP OSCAR 2 made up of 10 Marines and 20–30 Bru. They were located in their own little fortified area about 200 yards west on Highway 9.

Tying these elements together with U.S. firepower was CPT Clarke's challenge. The enemy would be relentless in its assault for the next 24 hours during which time CPT Clarke orchestrated the fight. After the telephone line had been severed—probably by a mortar or artillery round—in order to stay in communication with his advisors and monitor the general status of his little force, he was regularly moving throughout the area, exposing himself to a barrage of bullets with each venture around the compound. After each of these trips he and CPT Nhi conferred and strategized to maintain the integrity of the compound and to repulse the invading NVA. The two of them proved to be quite a team in defending the compound and defeating a foe much larger than their small force.

SGT Balanco was also moving throughout the compound and repositioning the CAP Marines to counter threats. He reported into the command bunker intermittently, as he was able.

By 7 AM, the fight that had started at 5:30 AM on that very foggy January morning, was reaching its critical point. The fog was still so thick that every individual felt his position was isolated from his comrades and the enemy could get dangerously close. The focus of the NVA attack was a pathway of vulnerability between the fort and compound behind the moat on the southwest side of the compound, outside the French Fort. The pagoda blocked observation there, making it the weakest area of the compound. Its limited visibility made easy access for the NVA and if they could breach the area that would put them quickly in center of the compound. Protecting that area was the job of the under-strength 915th Regional Forces (RF) Company.

The two exhausted platoons from the 915th RF Company were under constant attack on the beleaguered southwest side. The RFs were fatigued and needed support. SGT Balanco, after conferring with LT Stamper quickly moved two Marines, Lance Corporals Howard McKinnis and C. E. "Butch" Still, back to the French Fort with them. These two Marines were very brave and inspirational to all that observed them. Their presence and their large volume of fire were to stem the tide on the western side of the French Fort and to give the Vietnamese new energy.

Balanco was later awarded the Silver Star for his gallantry.

CPT Clarke was busy calling artillery and brought it in virtually right on top of the defenders—where the NVA were. The overhead cover on the bunkers that they had worked on to keep from collapsing during the rains served them well. They protected the occupants of the bunkers from the devastating effects of the shrapnel of artillery being fired in the variable time mode—where it exploded in the air and blew shrapnel down on everything exposed on the ground.

The NVA had launched a ferocious ground attack into the western edge of Khe Sanh village. After the initial assault was broken at about 8:30 AM the enemy simply backed off, and beginning around 9:00 AM or so they attempted to destroy the key bunkers in the French Fort by recoilless rifle and B40 rocket fire. Simultaneously they moved into Khe Sanh village and set up mortars near the dispensary with which they attempted to shell the compound. At this time, the police station was still communicating and this made it possible to put effective artillery and mortar fire on the enemy. The Vietnamese Police held the area and the NVA did not get in. CPT Nhi was able to put mortar fire from the 915th's mortar in that area with the direction of the police.

SFC Perry continues:

> Throughout the day I fired at muzzle flashes just peppering the rounds in. No way I could have missed every time, so I'm sure I took a few out. Many muzzle flashes were very close together, like the NVA were almost hugging one another. When we were out there counting bodies the next day and getting war trophies I found that several of these dead NVA were just kids—17 to 20 years old. They huddled close to one another while firing at us because they were scared. They now fully realized their field commanders had lied to them. No one welcomed them with open arms and we Americans and our Vietnamese and Bru counterparts were not lazy, listless, out of shape, or badly trained. Throughout the subsequent few hours we were able to continually bring fire to bear from our central bunker when and where it was needed. Initially, we kept Captain Clarke advised as to what was happening by telephone.

To Perry's front, Marine CPL Russell manning an M-60 machine gun stacked up NVA in front of his position like cord wood. His effort, and those of the other CAP Marines, was critical to stemming the initial and subsequent attacks.

SFC Perry, who throughout the battle exposed himself to heavy fire moving from bunker to bunker, pulled injured Vietnamese soldiers out of collapsed bunkers and then tended to their wounds.

Prados and Stubbe in their *Valley of Decision: The Siege of Khe Sanh* report, quoting LT Tom Stamper:

> I had told the Montagnards to keep down, but some of them by the main entrance didn't and were killed. Despite the heavy artillery the enemy kept attacking the perimeter. We took a lot of sniper fire from the pagoda, where it appeared the dead and wounded were being taken. We knocked that out by artillery—on the third round. We took a lot of fire from the 'bus stop' right outside the main entrance and brought in some "quick action" fused 105s but they kept sniping. We also took some small arms fire from the Howard Johnson's across the street and knocked them out. There appeared to be a blocking force by the entrance to the gate of the perimeter to prevent us from leaving the compound. We fired at least five hundred rounds of the RF's 60s, all without increments. They landed and exploded right outside our wires.

History records LT Stamper calling in artillery. This was not the case. Every artillery mission was called by CPT Clarke. Most of the artillery fire that was used was in two preplanned concentrations that MAJ Whitenack had coordinated prior to leaving and was executed by CPT Clarke to break up the attack. Both concentrations of artillery fire were two L-shaped concentrations of six guns firing and together they encircled the District Headquarters. The primary concentration was to the south of the compound and CPT Clarke was calling them in "danger close," risking the lives of friendly forces. The artillery Variable Time Fuse is more commonly referred to as fuse VT or just VT. VT allows the round to be set to detonate at a given distance in the air. This creates a barrage of shrapnel, but the occupants of a bunker with overhead cover were relatively safe from its effects. This meant that the artillery fire could be called very close to the compound without worry of injuring the defenders, which is exactly what CPT Clarke continually did.

George Amos, in his letter home to his wife, described this part of the battle:

> At exactly 5 AM the NVA attacked. We fired everything we had at them and they still kept coming. They went to the barbed concertina wire that surrounded the compound and were cutting it when our commander (Captain Clarke) called in artillery (105mm) on our own positions. Everything

was a mass of explosions and gunfire all around. This worked, and we held them off until daybreak.

CPT Clarke was calling fire from within a metal-walled bunker and could not trust his compass. He was making adjustments based on the gun target line rather than the azimuth (compass direction) to the target. Clarke dropped normal fire direction procedures and simplified them based on the location of the target and the location of the firing unit. The Marines at the Combat Base report that over a 1,000 rounds were fired in support of the District Headquarters.

Communications with the Province Headquarters at Quang Tri and the advisory team were marginal at best. Radio connections were combined and used in a Rube Goldberg arrangement that allowed CPT Clarke to maintain contact throughout the battle. Because of the spotty communications to Quang Tri, he coordinated with Special Forces at FOB-3 to provide radio relay back to Quang Tri from their operators on Hill 950. He would send them a message; they would copy it down and send it out on a different frequency to Quang Tri. Working in reverse with the response they were able to complete the circle of communications. It was a complicated system and certainly not optimal for instant and critical communication but it worked. Additionally, Special Forces channels through both Lang Vei and FOB–3 directly to Danang were used to finesse the system. He had one radio for communicating with the Marines for fire support, one for talking to Quang Tri, and once air strikes began, he had another talking to the pilot. The Vietnamese also had a single band radio that they used.

SFC Perry remembers details of that morning:

> After about 10 AM when the telephone line failed, Captain Clarke made regular trips under fire from the Command Bunker to our bunker to check our status and get a personal feel for what was occurring in the front half of the compound. His arrival and departure were frequently greeted by a fresh concentration of fire at the bunker. It was like the bullets were chasing him. After each of his visits we could almost always expect a new barrage of artillery fire at just the right time and spot.

The combination of radio and telephone reports that CPT Nhi was receiving, SGT Balanco's reports, and CPT Clarke's own reconnaissance provided the defenders with a fairly clear picture of what was occurring in the fog that was all around them.

During the next two hours the attempts by the NVA to penetrate the compound continued. The presence of Corporals McKinnis and Still and SGT Balanco's periodic visits were critical in stemming the NVA assault. SGT Balanco received one of his purple hearts for wounds suffered during one such effort. Each time that the NVA regrouped and attacked they were met by a mixture of fire from the small Vietnamese and Marine force and the artillery called by CPT Clarke.

SFCs Perry, King, and Kasper from the MACV bunker had a wide selection of weapons to engage the attackers with and a cache of ammunition. Situated above and behind all of the bunkers on the perimeter they could react to threats against any part of the front, or northern third of the compound and provide reinforcing fires to those on the perimeter. Their reinforcing fire and presence reassured the Bru and Marine defenders and added depth to what was otherwise a very linear fight—one that was really only one bunker or person deep. The front part of the compound was never as vulnerable to breaching as was the seam to the rear, between the French Fort and the District Compound. However, Corporal Russell would not agree with this statement as he killed more than 30 NVA in front of his machine gun position.

George Amos described the rest of the day as one of frustration "... the NVA (2 battalions—1,000 men) had us completely surrounded, and we received mortar rounds all day as well as sporadic sniper fire."

THE WESTERN APPROACH TO THE VILLAGE—
CAC-OSCAR 2'S FIGHT

While the major fight was going on around the District Headquarters, a separate, but critical, fight was occurring several hundred meters west of the District Headquarters. The efforts of CAC-OSCAR 2 were critical, as they protected the western approaches to the village and the District Headquarters. Without their heroic defensive efforts the compound would have fallen. The CAC-OSCAR 2 Marines consisted of: Dan Sullivan, CPL Harper, Frank Batchman, Jimmy Tyson, PFC Gullickson, PFC Biddle, PFC Dana Matonias, and Navy Corpsman John Roberts (who treated nine of the wounded) and several Bru. Corpsman Roberts was in the ambiguous situation of treating the dying and wounded, but doing his share of the killing to stay alive.

Corpsman John Roberts describes the fight at CAP OSCAR:

Early, before dawn, we could hear the eerie sound of rocket and artillery fire pounding the Khe Sanh Combat Base. At first, we thought it was all out-going interdiction fire, but radio traffic began to alert us to the ugly truth that a momentous event was about to begin in earnest—THE SIEGE OF KHE SANH, 77 days of death and destruction.

The District Headquarters and OSCAR 1 came under attack first, and of course we were monitoring all radio traffic which moments later confirmed the beginning of a full-scaled battalion or Regimental sized-sized

NVA ground attack. Every Marine and Popular Forces fighter at OSCAR 2 was ready and in his assigned fighting position.

The Bru were instructed to protect a sector on our left flank coming from the Khe Sanh village. Additionally, they were to re-load M-16 magazines for the Marines, who were to do most of the fighting. They performed well and we did not doubt their loyalty to us. After all, who knew more than the Bru about the mind-set of these few proud Marines? We had lived, worked, and patrolled together for many months. They had seen first hand how much the Marines had done for their people when no one else seemed to care very much. It was a mutual admiration. They had earned our respect, a respect not easily earned by others who are not Marines. It was this type of respect that set the Army advisors and CAP Marines aside from the average Marine and his leadership at the Combat Base. This mutual respect and the resultant cooperation was to a have an impact on this fight and the overall battle.

When the assault first hit it was preceded by an RPG round on the bunker next to Route 9 manned by two Marines, CPL Sullivan and PFC Gullickson. Sullivan fought like a madman, firing first with his M-16, then a Browning Automatic Rifle (BAR) while Gullickson re-loaded over and over.

SGT Harper rushed into the bunker from the trench-line and was immediately hit with shrapnel from a rocket propelled grenade. He was hit pretty badly just below the left eye and he suffered multiple wounds of a lesser degree. Gullickson shouted; "Corpsman up!" Fast application of a pressure bandage temporarily stopped the bleeding. Harper said gruffly; "Get out of my face Doc, I've got work to do—catch me later!"

The barrage of small arms fire, already fierce, was getting louder. Sullivan was sweeping his sector with automatic fire and "cleaning up" on the bad guys. They finally decided to bypass him and move around to the front of the compound where they faced not one but two automatic weapons (a BAR and an M-60). The entire perimeter erupted in gunfire, with NVA rocket propelled grenades (RPGs) aimed at every bunker and automatic weapons position. The NVA seemed to know our compound and its armament as well as we did. This was especially unnerving. With barely an hour gone by, all of my Marines were wounded to some degree. In the second hour I was able to give more definitive treatment to the Platoon Sergeant, SGT Harper. He had lost a lot of blood and needed a highball (which he would have preferred), or a serum albumin blood volume expander. He got the latter.

LCPL Jimmy Tyson received a serious wound to his left leg just above the knee. The NVA didn't know it, but for a short while, had they pushed their attack harder, in those early hours, we could have been over-run. Although every Marine was doing all that he could, most had wounds that were at least distracting and at worst life threatening.

As the corpsman, I cared for the injured, but of necessity, was required to take up weapons and fire from each gun position in an effort to make it seem that we were still at 100%. On one occasion, on the right flank, PFC Biddle and PFC Gullickson asked me to throw a couple of hand grenades to help break up an attack on their sector. I did, but the results were not all together satisfactory, as they both received superficial shrapnel wounds. In fact, they asked me not to throw any more until the next war. One yelled, "Doc, whose side are you on anyway?"

Our prior planning for this assault put us in a much-improved position to defend our compound. We had more open fields of fire with better visibility.

Throughout the morning Khe Sanh Combat Base provided us artillery support through Captain Clarke's skillful adjustments based on skimpy radio communications. I've often wondered how he could get that artillery so close to us and not hit us. I later learned that he was constantly moving the artillery around to ring the defenders with deadly steel based upon his own observations and sketchy information. That man must have had a unique ability to picture what was going on around him. We had no knowledge of much of what was happening, especially at the higher command levels. He was definitely getting it close!

During the first few hours of fighting, (the ferocity of which was a most terrifying experience), we began to wonder if we would be able to live up to our own bravado. We couldn't help but wonder if the Marines at the Combat Base were as troubled as we were. How could we (nine Marines, one corpsman, and ten or so Bru Popular Force troops) hold out until relief came, against at least a battalion, and perhaps a regiment, of NVA?

Throughout the day water was carefully rationed. Our only source of water was a Lister bag, a canvas water-storage device. Each time one of us tried to get to the water, snipers fired. Our ammunition was running low and we knew time and ammo would decide our fate. Frustration was mounting, profanity was the norm, and the demons of the foggy darkness that was this morning were having a field day.

AIR STRIKES TAKE THEIR TOLL

CPT Clarke knew his beleaguered forces could not hold out much longer without some reinforcements or backup. LT Stamper called for help from the Combat Base but Lounds told him it just wasn't possible to send a relief force to the village; he did, however, help out with more artillery fire. But artillery fire alone was not enough.

Around noon Regional Forces and Popular Forces were running low on ammunition (they were not known for their fire discipline) and CPT Clarke made the first of several ammunition resupply requests from the Combat Base. The Regional Forces and Popular Forces were armed with carbines,

M-1 rifles and 30 caliber machine guns—old Korean War vintage weapons. The Marines were armed with M-16s and M-60 machine guns. In short, the Combat Base didn't have the right kind of ammunition to resupply the local forces and initially denied the request.

The Special Forces at FOB–3 arranged to get the ammo and gave it to Marine helicopter pilots to deliver. The Marine choppers attempted to land in the landing zone behind the compound but took heavy fire. They aborted and were heading back to the Combat Base when CPT Clarke requested that they simply fly over the front of the compound and kick the ammo out. To this request one of the pilots answered that "he wasn't no fucking bombardier." Another pilot was less caustic and did drop some ammo that helped to partially relieve the problem. The helicopters returned to the Combat Base.

Around noon, Brewer and CPT Clarke both called for execution of the promised relief contingency plan that the Marines at the Combat Base had developed. A company from the base was finally dispatched to relieve the District Headquarters. The relief column had some ammunition for the local forces with it, which was badly needed. When the company reached Hill 471 and was able to look down on the village several kilometers away, the company commander called CPT Clarke and told him that his compound was surrounded, to which Clarke responded "no shit!" The commander informed Clarke that they were under orders to return to the Combat Base. CPT Clarke never received any word of the Marine Company receiving any incoming fire, however George Amos recalled:

> A company of Marines set out from the base (5 miles away) on foot to reach us but were forced to go back because they ran out of ammo trying to get to us.
>
> We remained in our bunker all day, and then at dusk they told us the *bad* news—NO reinforcements or ammo could be brought to us and we would have to last the night. We were very, very short on ammo and we all thought we would not make it thru the night.
>
> So far during the day we had 6 of our men killed and about 1/2 were wounded, at least slightly. We were monitoring their (NVA) radio and we heard them call for 2 battalions to reinforce them. The situation looked very hopeless and we could only sit and stare into the darkness and tremble with fear. We knew that if they attacked again that we were finished, as nighttime hampers air support.

Throughout the assault Clarke had kept in contact with Brewer at the Province Headquarters. What Clarke needed was air strikes and Brewer was determined that he get them.

The air effort started as the fog began to burn off. Initially a Marine Forward Air Controller (FAC) put in two flights of jets that reduced the sniping activity significantly. At the end of that air strike the pilot told CPT Clarke that that was all that he could do for him. Fortunately, communications continued with Quang Tri and CPT Clarke was able to get more FAC support from the Province Advisory Team. CPT Ward Britt, an Air Force FAC working out of Quang Tri, flew below the clouds and between mountaintops to get to Khe Sanh to coordinate the air strikes. All afternoon he controlled numerous air strikes on the massed NVA who were trying to reorganize and reassault the compound. He diverted fighter pilots from their bombing missions over the Ho Chi Minh Trail to come in and drop ordnance to protect the small garrison. The fog gave the enemy the advantage by concealing their location but the bravery of the pilots to fly below ceiling negated that advantage. One F-4 was shot down but the pilot was rescued. On one of these air strikes the FAC put in two fighters on 100 NVA in the open and after it was over he could not see any movement—just bodies.

Ward Britt remembers the afternoon of air strikes:

> The 01-E, FAC aircraft, only carried 4 rockets, but I happened to have smoke grenades on board so I used them to mark targets during the fighter strikes. With all the ground fire I never took a hit. It was very unusual for fighters to agree to work below a cloud deck but all did so with no hesitation.

The recommendation for the Silver Star for CPT Britt tells the story much more completely and demonstrates the interaction between him and the advisory team and the use of radio intercept data by the District Forces to decimate more than a company:

> While on a routine afternoon reconnaissance mission Captain Britt was informed that the Huong Hoa District Headquarters was under heavy ground attack and in danger of being overrun by a regimental-size hostile force. While proceeding into the rugged mountain area he made contact with Captain Clarke, the senior sector advisor, and was advised that the headquarters compound was surrounded and taking continuous automatic weapons and mortar fire. He was also advised that an A-4 had been shot down by hostile ground fire only a few minutes before. There was a scattered broken cloud deck at 2000 feet, which was to hamper air operations for the rest of the day.
>
> As Captain Britt came on the scene he relayed Captain Clarke's request for immediate air strikes. Captain Britt saw from 300 to 500 troops in the open and in hastily dug positions within 200 meters of the outer perimeter of the Huong Hoa District Headquarters.
>
> As the fighters arrived he briefed them on the situation and the friendly and hostile positions. Khe Sanh village was immediately north of the headquarters so all of the strikes were concentrated on the south side while the artillery from Khe Sanh Combat Base supported the village.

The first fighters were directed to place their 750 pound bombs 300 meters south of the perimeter and Captain Britt methodically directed the bombs closer on each pass so that the last bombs were going off less than 200 meters from the besieged compound. Both the fighters and Captain Britt came under heavy automatic weapons fire throughout the strike.

After the strike Captain Clarke advised that they had intercepted a hostile radio message calling for reinforcement and a full company of medics and stretcher-bearers. Captain Britt flew into the area of the approaching reinforcements and was able to locate their positions. During this visual reconnaissance Captain Britt received sporadic small arms fire but continued with his mission.

He directed the second set of fighters against the reinforcing troops and all aircraft again came under heavy automatic weapons fire. His precision in directing this strike so effectively neutralized these reinforcing troops that they never reached the vicinity of the headquarters compound.

With his third set of fighters Captain Britt again concentrated on the area immediately south of the District Headquarters and Captain Clarke reported he could see troops withdrawing from that area during and after the strike.

By this time it was almost dark and Captain Britt was out of rockets. Captain Clarke requested one more strike on suspected mortar positions to minimize the effectiveness of the hostile forces during the coming night. Captain Britt made another reconnaissance flight over hostile territory, still drawing small arms fire, and was able to locate and mark two mortar positions with smoke grenades for his fifth set of fighter aircraft.

Captain Britt was forced to land at the Khe Sanh airbase to refuel before returning to his home station. He had remained in an area of intense hostile small arms and automatic weapons fire for more than three and one half hours; he had directed five separate flights of fighter aircraft against hostile targets, deliberately exposing himself to heavy automatic weapons at low altitude to locate and mark these targets.

From about 1 PM on for the rest of the daylight hours there were three simultaneous activities going on in the compound—coordination of air strikes and other reinforcing activities, consolidation of the compound's defenses, supply, and redistribution of ammunition and water.

There were several other attempts to breach the fortifications in the area between the back of the pagoda and the RF fort. One of those attempts occurred while CPT Clarke was surveying the damage to the bunker that dominated that point. There were several NVA providing suppressive fire while a sapper tried to crawl forward and place a charge up against the bunker to destroy it. CPT Clarke shot him with a high explosive round from his M79 grenade launcher. The sapper's body was severed in two, though the parts continued to try and crawl forward. The pagoda was also a constant source of harassing fire. The CAC-OSCAR Marines used Light Anti-Tank Weapons (LAWs) to blow holes through its cement walls. The resulting spalling and shrapnel killed the snipers. However, they were replaced several times and the process was resumed.

CPT Clarke's main focus during the afternoon hours was working with CPT Nhi to develop targets and then to guide CPT Britt to the areas where they thought that he would find more NVA. Britt reported that almost every time he put an air strike in he found more NVA and that he was have a devastating effect on the enemy. It seemed that Clarke always had at least two or three radio nets working at any one time.

By this time the fog had lifted and visibility was clear. But a fog much heavier then any nature can call soon enwrapped the compound and the men that were to come to her rescue. The fog of war coupled with the lack of unity of command was about to take a greater toll than the NVA.

CPT Clarke had called for relief all during the battle. The first two attempts, the helicopter resupply and the Marine relief company from the Fire Base, had not been successful. The air strikes had relieved the compound somewhat but he still needed ammo, supplies, and reinforcements. As CPT Britt was leaving the Khe Sanh area he encountered a Black Cat helicopter relief formation that was on its way in. The helicopter pilot, CW2 Pullen, radioed Britt who told him, "Turn around and go back or you will die."

Chapter 8

BLACK CATS TO THE RESCUE

There are multiple views of what happened during the attempts by the 282nd Light Helicopter Company to resupply and reinforce the beleaguered Khe Sanh District Headquarters garrison on January 21, 1968, demonstrating how history can be inaccurately recorded. This chapter chronicles the events as they happened in the words of the participants, leaving to history a more accurate, detailed account. The relief efforts by the Black Cats culminated in a disastrous combat assault against the Old French Fort, site of FOB-3, to the east of Khe Sanh village, on the late afternoon of the January 21, 1968. This failed assault highlights the fog and friction of war. Unity of command would have meant that there was unity of effort. All of the various units involved would have been working as part of a team with a common and shared goal. This, of course, was not the case. The Marines had abandoned the relief mission, which necessitated that the Province Headquarters at Quang Tri had to attempt to provide aid. The relief missions it dispatched were not informed of the presence of the enemy and CPT Clarke was at the mercy of tenuous communications and a relentless foe working hard to invade the compound. Bob Brewer, the province chief advisor, thought that the relief flight was going in behind the Khe Sanh District Headquarters. LTC Seymoe, his deputy accompanying the flight, took it in another direction. Compounding these elements was the veil of secrecy and stealth prior to the battles. All these factors contributed to things not going as one might have wished.

The lack of unity of command and focus contributed to the fog of war and the resulting loss of life. The helicopters were ambushed as they attempted to set down and the force was mauled. LTC Seymoe lost his life in this effort—as did a number of other valiant soldiers.

In spite of the command disunity the soldiers on the ground responded to positive leadership. They fought gallantly and deserve recognition for the hardships and agony they endured. The media would lead you to believe that all Vietnam veterans are psychologically scarred and were against the war. This brief episode demonstrates that the soldiers of this effort were dedicated and loyal to the job at hand and their stalwart efforts were ultimately rewarded with a victory. There were no examples of "fragging" or other unsoldierly behavior during this entire battle. The entire event was replete with brave Americans doing what they were trained to do, willing to sacrifice everything for their comrades, and unwilling to quit until the job was done. Witness Black Cat door gunner Jerry Elliott jumping from his helicopter to help other company mates and who in doing so was lost forever, now counted among the missing in action (MIA). There were John Balanco, Jim Perry, and John Roberts putting themselves at risk to care for their comrades. Lastly were CPT Clarke and SFC King forgoing aerial evacuation to care for their Vietnamese and Bru comrades.

THE BLACK CATS

The combat assault mission was executed by the helicopters of the 282nd Air Mobile Light Helicopter Company (AML), the Black Cats. First activated at Fort Benning, Georgia, on October 7, 1965, the company deployed personnel, aircraft, and equipment, arriving at Marble Mountain Airfield in Danang in the late spring of 1966. They flew missions in I and II Corps (the northern part of South Vietnam) in support of MACV, Special Forces, Long Range Reconnaissance Patrols (LRRP), Ranger, and Hac Bao units (the name given to an elite group of hardcore, highly trained and spirited Vietnamese fighting men—all-volunteer companies of special mission ARVN soldiers). The wide range of support rendered to I and II Corps necessitated company personnel and aircraft to be garrisoned throughout South Vietnam. Ten aircraft were assigned to I Corps, two at Hue Citadel, two at Quang Ngai and six at Danang. Sixteen aircraft were assigned to II Corps, eight each at Pleiku and An Son.

The unit performed a great variety of missions, carrying in its 26 assigned aircraft passengers that ranged from prisoners of war to military and government VIPs and cargo from medical supplies and ammunition to live animals for food supplies. Crews consisted of an aircraft commander, pilot, crew chief, and gunner. They flew medevacs, combat assaults, LRRP insertions and extractions; delivered hot food to troops fighting in rough terrain; delivered water, ammo, mail, batteries, and beer to Special Forces base camps, artillery observation posts, or any other type of mission which was required. Normal combat assaults involved hauling ARVN troops with the Black Cats as lead elements followed by ARVN helicopters, followed by USMC (United States Marine Corps) helicopters. They sustained more than their share of casualties.

The 282nd flew UH-1 (Huey) helicopters and consisted of three flight platoons. First and Second Flight Platoons flew lift helicopters (Slicks) armed with an M-60 machinegun on each side. The Third Flight Platoon flew heavily armed UH-1B's and C's gunships.

WO Paul Callaway, one of the pilots leading the gunship support element of the ill-fated relief attempt, described the nature of a heavy fire team:

> Our UH1B's were armed with four flex-mounted M-60 machine guns, two per side, mounted on pilot-activated pylons. We carried about 3,000 rounds for these in internally mounted trays. Each aircraft had fourteen 2.75" folding fin aerial rockets with ten pound warheads (about the power of 2/3 of a 105 howitzer round) plus two door gunners sporting M-60 free-mounted machine guns. The Frog was a derivative of the UH1B mounting, the M3 aerial 40mm grenade launcher. This was a turret-mounted, low-velocity launcher, which packed quite a punch on troops in the open. It lobbed the grenades (the grenades were similar to the M-79 shoulder fired but about 2–3 times the kill power) at about 250 rounds per minute, to a range of about 700 yards. Firing this thing was like throwing a softball—very slow velocity must be combined with a high trajectory in order to hit what you were aiming at. It was not much of a direct-fire weapon, kind of like a mortar. We carried about 350 rounds in an internal mounted feeder tray. This version also mounted thirty-six 2.75 rockets in two 18-shot pods—one per side. When fully loaded this entire affair was about 500 pounds more than the aircraft was designed to lift.
>
> In order to get these flying rocks airborne, we would take off from the airport with the door gunners running along the side. As the aircraft settled for its first bounce the crew would jump on board. As we hit the second bounce (about 7–9 knots) the aircraft would lumber into the air, and on the third bounce (effective translational lift at about 12 to 14 knots) we would be flying. Meanwhile the low rpm audio system was beeping as loud as it can to tell you that you were about to crash. This was the procedure if you intended to have enough ordnance and fuel on board to do anybody any good on arrival.
>
> And we did good! We were the only Army aviation assets in I Corps for most of 1967–1968. We were very good at close air-support for the ground units. The Marine grunts loved to see us coming as we were allowed to get

down and dirty with the enemy where the Marine assets were restricted by regulation to break off attacks under 1,000 feet. We also did a lot of night attack work under flares or with the light ship providing illumination. It was a very exciting time for a 20 year old. During my time with the gunships of the 282 I received 2 Distinguished Flying Crosses and an Air Medal with Valor device, which I got for that day at Khe Sanh.

The 282nd aviators conducted their missions in weather that demanded the very highest form of flying discipline. The Black Cats flew sortie after sortie through extremely poor weather conditions to accomplish their vital missions in support of the I Corps Advisory effort. Their bravery is undisputed, their tenacity to task unparalleled.

THE COMBAT ASSAULT

From the beginning of the attack on the compound CPT Clarke continually updated his province advisor, Bob Brewer, that his landing zone (LZ) at the District Compound, was "hot." He needed reinforcements and supplies but he needed ammunition in the worst way. He told Brewer he could maybe hold out for another day if he had ammo. Through the intensity of battle he managed to keep in contact with Brewer, relying on the radio relay on Hill 950. He suggested that it might be possible to land at the Old French Fort east of the village. Brewer's promise to blow down the coffee trees at the plantation for a clearer landing hadn't happened, making it impossible to land there with any safety.

Brewer called for a resupply effort from the Hue Citadel airfield. LTC Seymoe, his deputy senior province advisor, was to lead the effort in resupplying the compound. LTC Seymoe was a Korean War veteran with 17 years in service. Although he was certainly fit for service, he had been wounded in the head during Korea and had a hearing problem. The hearing problem, along with the lack of sufficient communication, could very well have been the seed of the resultant disorganization. LTC Seymoe was not talking to the Marine artillery and CPT Clarke was not sure exactly what LTC Seymoe was doing. They had little communication. The result was a catastrophe.

The relief effort was lead by a UH1 helicopter, piloted by Chief Warrant 2 (CW2) Officer Pullen. Onboard were CW2 Gilmore and Crew Chief Seghetti. A second helicopter was piloted by CW McKinsey. In route CW2 Pullen radioed Ward Britt, the Air Force FAC, who was putting in air strikes at the compound, and told him what they were attempting to do. Ward Britt advised them to turn back because the target was so hot.

CW2 Pullen, the Black Cat pilot, recalls the first attempt to resupply the compound:

The morning of 21 January, 1968, began normally enough ... I took off from the Hue Citadel airfield rather late in the morning, as I recall, and was directed to land at La Vang airfield, near Quang Tri, to pick up ammunition, medical supplies, and water, and to deliver these supplies to Khe Sanh Village.

I was not briefed about any enemy activity in the area, and was unaware that Khe Sanh Village was under siege. I landed at La Vang and picked up the cargo, as well as two Vietnamese enlisted men, three stretchers for medevacs, and LTC Seymoe. There may have been one other American passenger, I'm not sure. I flew to Khe Sanh, contacted their HQ on the radio, and was cleared to land. No reports of enemy activity in that part of the compound.

I determined that the wind was from the south, flew to the north of the compound and set up a normal approach to the single ship LZ outside the camp perimeter. The LZ was carved out of some tall trees, which surrounded it on three sides, and the west side of the LZ bordered the camp perimeter.

I was about 50 feet from touchdown, in a rather steep approach, when I saw a soldier in olive drab fatigue uniform step from the southern tree line, in plain view of the camp, point his weapon directly at my aircraft, and begin to fire. Since my airspeed was only about 20 knots, evasive action consisted of diving the aircraft beyond the LZ into the valley to gain airspeed and maneuvering capabilities.

As I cleared the LZ, my crew chief, Seghetti, informed me that he had been hit in the foot. I saw several green tracers (The NVA's tracer rounds were a distinctive green in color while US tracers were red/orange in color. Usually every 5th round in belt of machine gun ammunition would be a tracer round.) pass the nose of the aircraft as I pulled up to gain altitude, and I extended my low level flight until I was out over the valley floor before I gained sufficient altitude to be safe from small arms fire. The radio operator (Clarke) at Khe Sanh called on FM and said that he was unaware that there were enemy in the LZ, that he was sorry about us getting shot up, and that we had better not try another approach until the LZ was cleared.

I went through a series of turning maneuvers to check my controls, turned to a course for Quang Tri, and let my pilot, WO Gilmore, take the controls. I inquired about the condition of crew chief Seghetti, and LTC Seymoe replied that he was administering first aid to him, and that the bullet had gone clean through his foot and he had controlled the bleeding.

This third attempt at relief was frustrating for all involved. CPT Clarke was unaware that the landing zone was surrounded. These continual setbacks were demoralizing, and leaving the compound with an increased sense of desperation. At this point there had been three relief efforts, only one of which had been partially successful. The inability to supply these men was frustrating to Quang Tri as well as in the village. Pullen continues:

> LTC Seymoe asked if I could contact the 282nd HQ at Danang and get more helicopters sent up to assist in a combat assault to relieve Huong Hoa, and I called my Section Leader, Lieutenant (LT) Robert Ford, to inform him of our situation and the request for additional support. LT Ford advised that he had also taken fire from the LZ at Huong Hoa, Khe Sanh, was on his way to Quang Tri, and would coordinate the requested support with the 282nd. I informed LTC Seymoe that I would land at La Vang airfield, because they had an aid station there, and Seghetti needed medical attention. Seymoe used the aircraft radio to coordinate with his staff.
>
> After landing at La Vang, I immediately shut down and inspected the aircraft for damage. There were two small caliber bullet holes in the left "wheel well" where Seghetti had been sitting, and six holes in the cargo compartment and tail boom. A thorough inspection revealed a minor bullet strike on the left side of the main transmission, and two bullet holes in the engine firewall. I retrieved an armor-piercing bullet core from the engine deck, which I gave to Seghetti. The red liquid leaking profusely from the rear of the aircraft was traced to a case of transmission fluid in the cargo compartment, which had taken two rounds. The aircraft was flyable.

CW2 McKinsey, piloting the other helicopter, felt that the mission needed to be completed. Pullen remembers that he, McKinsey:

> ... had an idea to go to Dong Ha to get fuel and he wanted to ask the Marine helicopter unit to help us complete this mission. When we landed at Dong Ha, there was a Marine officer standing by one of the helicopters. Mr. McKinsey went over and talked to the Marine. When Mr. McKinsey came back over to where we were, he indicated that the Marines would be unable to help us for some reason. I was pretty nervous about going back to Khe Sanh due to all the heavy fire we had taken earlier. I told him that if we went back somebody was going to get hurt.
>
> LTC Seymoe really wanted to get the supplies delivered. Mr. McKinsey then called Danang to apprise Major Ward (the Company Commander) and Captain Stiner (the Operations Officer) of the situation. I sure would have liked to have heard that conversation! That is when the rest of the Black Cats were dispatched from Danang to Quang Tri. This is when LTC Seymoe requested more ARVN troops to go along on the next trip to Khe Sanh.

Seymoe's two helicopters in Quang Tri were soon joined by seven others coming from Danang. One of the pilots was CPT Stiner, the Operations Officer of 282nd Attack Helicopter Company. CPT Stiner remembers:

I received the request as Operations Officer for the 282d at approximately 1300 hours. The formal request we received at about 1400 hours and by 1500 hours I took four D models (guns), left Danang and started north for Quang Tri with the intention of rendezvousing with 3 other Delta models that I already had operating in the area. Major Rex and I were flying the lead aircraft.

Warrant Officer McKinsey' had been flying in that area all morning. He had flown over this old French fort for approximately 2 hours at various altitudes. He further had operated up there for the past 11 months. With his knowledge of the area, having already been in there the same day, he volunteered to fly in the lead aircraft with me. So he changed places with Major Rex who went back and took the seat that McKinsey had previously occupied.

Although the engines were now turning for the relief mission that was so badly needed, the vital element missing was coordination. When asked why there was not a complete preparation of the landing zone by air and ground-delivered ordnance Paul Callaway, the warrant officer leading the gunship support element, stated:

Well, this was a point of dispute at the time. The Company Commander M. J. Ward took over the Combat Assault at the briefing at Danang and the whole thing was a shoddy, quick deal! NOBODY took charge. Normally, he let one of the experienced Slick leads do this job. First I knew of the flight was when I was called out to meet on the ramp with the company commander. They chose the old French Fort as the only place we could insert a whole company of slicks. I was given the task of organizing the armed helicopter support, but was not allowed to ask pertinent questions or make suggestions to the company commander. It was 'fire these puppies up and we will brief on company frequency' (in the air). I had a heavy fire team with two B model Hueys with the M60 kits and 7-shot pods. My ship was the Frog with the 40-mm launcher and 36 rockets. As I remember we took off from Danang and picked up the ARVN at Quang Tri. All the ARVN troops were standing around on the tarmac. It was the policy and the way we fire team leads were taught to be the point on arranging for artillery and air support. I was not allowed to do this. It is a shame and a lot of good troops, US and ARVN, were killed because of a rush that was not slowed down.

Major Ward briefed that the unit would be inserting a company of support troops into the area to support the advisory team at Khe Sanh. He gave a very short briefing and they looked at a map. They must have thought that the NVA were stupid and did not know that the Old French Fort was the only place a combat assault could be inserted in the area.

Upon arrival at Quang Tri the pilots were apprised of the situation. CPT Stiner remembers:

We were briefed in detail by a Lieutenant Colonel (LTC) Joseph Seymoe who was the Province Deputy Senior Advisor. We were informed of the situation.

Khe Sanh, the town itself and the MACV compound of Khe Sanh, had been under heavy attack since 0530 hours the same morning. They were reportedly surrounded by a regiment and the enemy had 50-caliber positions coverage for 360 degrees, at least 4 positions there. It was decided that it probably would be impossible to get the troops into Khe Sanh Village, which was their final destination. We were given an alternate landing site, an old fort called the Old French Fort. About 1200 meters due east of the city and compound of Khe Sanh.

LTC Seymoe wanted to ride on the lead aircraft also since there were no other American Advisors to go with this unit. He wanted to see where they went and all frequencies were coordinated and what have you.

CW2 Pullen was waiting at Quang Tri with LTC Seymoe:

While I was inspecting my aircraft, LT Ford had arrived and plans were well under way for a combat assault (CA) into Khe Sanh. Four UH-1D's from Danang, three UH-1D's from the Hue Section, including mine, and two UH-1C and one UH-1B Gunships would make up the assault force. Vietnamese RF troops were arriving by truck at the airfield, escorted by a USMC security force on Armored Personnel Carriers. I approached one of the Marines (PFC Brittingham) manning an M-60 machine gun on an APC and asked if he would like to man Seghetti's machine gun during the assault. After clearing the request with his Gunnery Sergeant, this young man took his station and received some instruction on working the gun from Sp/4 Payne.

LTC Seymoe returned to my ship to begin the Combat Assault (CA), and I pointed out to him that I had several thousand pounds of ammo on board, and suggested that he command the assault from another ship. He concurred, and boarded the helicopter being flown by Captain Tommy C. Stiner and WO Gerald L. McKinsey. Since I was the only ship not carrying troops, I was assigned chalk number 7, "Tail End Charlie," and was the last ship to take off from La Vang.

Vietnamese RF troops were loaded and preparations made to begin the assault.

Sergeant Billy Hill, who was killed in this effort, was a good friend of SP5 David Howington and agreed to fly on this mission this day so that the regular door gunner could go to a social engagement. CW2 McKinsey was scheduled to go home in just a couple of weeks. He had already moved from Hue back to Danang for this purpose.

The combat force of 10 UH-1 helicopters, seven lift helicopters escorted by three gunships, was now on its way to the Old French Fort. They were carrying 50 Regional Forces troops of the 256th RF Company to reinforce the compound, several thousand pounds of ammunition, medical supplies, 5-gallon cans of water, and cases of ammunition for the WWII vintage weapons that the PFs had. Although they were loaded with men and material the one thing they were not carrying was information or knowledge about what they were to do when they got there. What they did know was that they were losing light and that they must be quick in order to deliver their goods before dark.

THE NVA AWAIT

The NVA report that prior to the 7th Battalion, 66th Regiment, 304th Division's attack on Huong Hoa Subsector; the 9th Battalion, 304th Division, NVA sent one platoon to occupy the Ku Boc road junction. One other platoon was to occupy Hill 471. Orders were to hold these two features at all costs. The 9th Battalion of the 66th Regiment was placed close to Highway 9, prepared to attack any relief forces that might approach Huong Hoa subsector overland along Highway 9, from Tan Lam and Ca Lu, and to counter any attempt to insert relief forces by air assault in the area south and southeast of the Ku Boc road junction. The Ku Boc road junction is located approximately 1,000 meters north–northeast of the recorded crash site of Black Cat tail number 61027. NVA accounts also use the name Ku Boc to refer to the Old French Fort (a.k.a. FOB-3). It was here that the 11th Company laid in wait in deep trenches, undetectable from the air.

It was here that Tran Dinh Ky and his squad laid in wait. Ky had been given his orders. He was to get his squad into position to support the occupation of the Ku Boc road junctions by the 11th Company, of the 9th Battalion of the 66th Regiment. Ky himself would carry the most powerful weapon on his own back: a B-40 rocket propelled antitank grenade. It did not, however, make him feel immune to the "bronze candy," NVA slang for enemy bullets.

The NVA had the self-discipline not to engage earlier flights over the Fort and held their fire until the helicopters were committed to landing. The NVA thus created an opportunity for judgment error and were rewarded for their efforts.

ENROUTE TO KHE SANH

CW2 Pullen, who was flying gunship support, recalls the short flight from Quang Tri to Khe Sanh:

Enroute to the combat assault area, I had my gunner brief the two ARVN passengers about getting the ammo and water out in the Landing Zone

(LZ) as soon as possible after landing, and to make sure they were strapped in securely when we were airborne again . . . I was not privy to any of the planning for the CA, nor was I aware of where the LZ was going to be. I simply followed the six aircraft in front of me, ready to descend and land whenever they did.

We flew in the direction of Khe Sanh, and meandered about in a loose staggered trail formation while the gunships strafed a bald hill East of the Huong Hoa compound.

[This statement illustrates a classic sample of the fog of war. All other accounts say that the gunships were not employed until after the ambush had occurred.]

I could see old building foundations of white concrete on the hill. I commented to Gilmore about the lack of ground fire (fire FROM the ground), and the lack of Air Force prep on the LZ (bombs on target), but figured my commanders knew what they were doing.

The formation soon tightened up, and began approaching the LZ . . .

ARRIVING AT THE LANDING ZONE AT THE OLD FRENCH FORT

CPT Stiner remembers the approach to the landing zone:

We circled this old French fort 360 degrees at a mean altitude of approximately 800 to 1,000 feet. Looked perfectly harmless, we determined to make a landing there, informed the MACV American Advisor who was over in Khe Sanh itself (Clarke). He agreed that that's where he wanted them and that there should be no activity there.

Gun ships made a good, thorough prep, [placed machine gun fire and rocket fire]. We established on a good final approach maneuvering around so that all the aircraft could fire. All door guns were delivering suppressive fire. Everything looked perfectly normal; we made the approach to the ground.

From Stiner's description of the events we know that the flight of helicopters flew over the French Fort and did not see any activity. Calloway had flown over the French Fort earlier and it had been unoccupied, or at least appeared that way. They also may have had gunships attempt to put suppressive fire into the area without drawing return fire, though there is a lot of disagreement about this.

Seymoe then ordered the slicks to land his relief force at the Old French Fort. That place, since the departure of FOB-3, had in the last day or so become an NVA stronghold. The NVA was dug in and camouflaged.

Seymoe directed the pilot, CPT Stiner, to land his helicopter at the Old French Fort position instead of the LZ in the District HQ compound and was immediately taken under heavy fire as some of the ARVN troops debarked.

The landing force of helicopters encountered no resistance during the gunship strike (if it occurred) or approach. Just as Stiner's skids touched down, however, the NVA stood up all around them. The ARVN troops had begun to off load. The entire platoon opened fire on the unsuspecting U.S. Army and ARVN soldiers. They opened up with machine guns (MG) and rocket-propelled grenades (RPGs) at close range The result was a massacre. CPT Stiner recalls:

McKinsey was flying to the ground and still on the controls at this time. I said words to the effect of "get out of here," more specifically I instructed SGT Hill, who was the gunner, and Sp5 Howington, who was the crew chief, that as soon as we picked- up over the edge of the ARVN for them to start shooting.

I know SGT Hill was in the aircraft at this time because I looked back. We picked up to approximately 8 feet, 8 to 10 feet of altitude, nosed the aircraft forward to get out of the area. At that time we were hit with what could have been any large caliber weapon—I suspect maybe a 57mm recoilless rifle. Could have been a direct hit by mortar, but there was reportedly some direct fire coming from the right side.

Specialist Howington agreed with CPT Stiner's description and added that the NVA started coming out of their fox holes like ants. Except for Ky, who waited patiently under cover for a clear shot with his antitank weapon. His target was an American UH-1 helicopter, tail number 027, CPT Stiner's ship. He stood, took careful aim, and fired. The B-40 round made a direct hit on the gunner's seat.

At that point all hell broke loose. The ARVN troops never had a chance. It was a killing zone. Fortunately, only a few aircraft got caught in the LZ ambush. Several were able to break off when the shooting started. If the NVA had waited another few seconds they would have gotten the whole company. Pullen saw Stiner's ship lifting off and a large explosion erupted from the right transmission well. Stiner's ship pitched forward violently, bursting into flames; even the rotor blades were burning as they slowly turned. The ship disappeared over the edge of the LZ. All glass was knocked out, rotor blades stopped, and the aircraft pitched forward and slid, upside down and burning, approximately 75 meters down the side of the hill.

CPT Stiner, who miraculously escaped injury, recalls the moments immediately after the explosion:

It (his helicopter) appeared to have buckled in the middle, with the tail and nose both falling down. Rotor blades stopped. We just had enough forward momentum to pitch on over the hill. As we pitched off over the embankment that gave us probably as much as 30 feet to fall. The aircraft was in flames at this time. It crashed into the ground about maybe 35 to

40 meters north of the perimeter that was occupied by the NVA and came to rest inverted. McKinsey and I crawled out through the windshield.

The side gunner, SGT Hill, was crushed and dead. The large round that knocked the ship down struck the aircraft at his position, probably instantly killing him. His machinegun was blown to pieces.

At this-point Warrant Officer Gerald McKinsey appeared to have sustained no injuries what-so-ever.

Stiner and WO McKinsey crawled out of the burning craft. CPT Stiner reports that he:

... took his carbine and started firing up the hill. There was a clearing that was not a road but could have been used as a trail about 6 or 8 feet wide where all the tall elephant grass had been mashed down. The NVA troops were storming down this portion, McKinsey took up a firing position, prone position, facing up the hill and commenced delivering fire. I saw the Colonel lying on his back, pinned under the aircraft, flames had not yet reached him. Seymoe was alive, but unconscious, pinned by an aluminum bar used to secure stretchers. The fire was spreading, ready to explode, and the NVA began to descend upon us. I ran to the Colonel's aid and attempted to free him. LTC Seymoe was still alive at this time or at least he blinked his eyes a couple of times; he didn't make a sound.

There were no apparent, no visible marks on him at all. Just appeared to be lying there pinned down. I tried to free him by lifting his arms—tugging at his belt, free one leg at a time—had no luck. A rescue aircraft, the second aircraft in formation, saw that we had crashed, did a 360 and was at the crash site seconds after we had crawled out of the airplane. The aircraft landed, and SP5 Danny Williams came to assist.

Sp5 Danny Williams hopped out of this aircraft and ran over to see if he could help us. When he arrived he came straight to me. He and I both tried to free the Colonel. He got one leg and I got the other leg. We couldn't free him, but I had determined by this time that the LTC Seymoe was dead. This is strictly a non-medical determination. His eyes were wide open and his eyes rolled back up into his head; there was no movement and no apparent breathing. I didn't feel his pulse or anything like this. The flames had gotten to his feet at this time. We left him. I crawled to McKinsey.

I had just gotten maybe 3 feet from McKinsey and started to take up a firing position with him, when he was struck in the back of the head. I have an idea it was a tracer because I could see the ball of fire enter his head as well as the splat and subsequent collapse. He fell over onto his chest, with his body weight on his head tumbling slightly down hill. I have no doubt that Gerald McKinsey died instantly at approximately 1745 on 21 January

'68. I also sent Spec5 Williams to crawl to his body and Spec 5 Williams verified that McKinsey was dead. I took his carbine crawled back out of the line of fire. Williams and I started firing in a different position.

Pvt. Elliott, gunner in the second aircraft to land and try to assist, ran to reach CPT Stiner to assist him along with the Crew Chief. In a matter of seconds, the Crew Chief returned to his aircraft and advised his pilot to takeoff, leaving Elliott on the ground.
CPT Stiner continues:

At the time I thought there were still 2 crewmembers, SGT Hill and Spec 5 Howington unaccounted for. I determined they were neither in nor under the ship. The compartment Howington occupied was in good shape so I had reason to believe he was around here. We found a hole at the rear of the aircraft, an indention in the earth of some type. Williams and I and one ARVN soldier got down in this hole. I gave Williams the rifle; he would cover me and I would crawl out different directions as far as I could and when I'd get detected and fired on I would crawl back into the hole. We did this for approximately four minutes.

They had gotten close enough to start throwing hand grenades in on us. We moved out to the rear, ran down the hill, escaped the enemy and continued to move throughout the night and joined the lines the next morning.

CW2 Callaway, in command of the supporting gunships, remembers those fiery events and the very dangerous and unscripted landings:

I again asked for permission to call up artillery or air and was denied because of time. It's getting dark. Why? Who knows? Probably because the Major didn't want to take advice from a 20-year-old warrant officer.

I don't think that anybody coordinated with the fire control at Khe Sanh at all. We circled the fort about three times. I had briefed the commander that as our gunships were much slower than the Slicks we would need time to position our aircraft before the flight turned final–approached for a landing.

Needless to say the flight lead turned inside of our covering aircraft without notice. I ended up with two aircraft almost hovering on the right and one aircraft trying to fly fast enough to catch up on the left— neither worked. The flight was on short final before a single gunship could be brought to bear.

They made their landing without a single shot of covering fire or suppressive cover. The NVA opened up with machine guns and rocket propelled grenades at close range. I don't remember the exact number of aircraft shot down in the Landing Zone (LZ). But we lost at least one and several so damaged they had to land at the Khe Sanh Combat Base. After about 8 to 10 minutes I made a low pass under fire and could not see any living "friendlies". I, in frustration, brought my entire team into attack position and assaulted the LZ with rockets and MG and 40 millimeter grenades. We laid down all we had on the area. These pilots and crew were the best! I had worked with them for most of my tour. We were young but we did know our trade and were very good at it.

This tragedy would not have happened if the crews had been allowed to do their jobs and the commander had not been in such a big hurry. A little thought and preparation would have saved lives. We tried!!! After this diabolical event we worked in the Khe Sanh area during the whole battle and through the Tet offense. I was later told that that barrage enabled our S-1 and two crewmembers, plus one ARVN, to break out of certain capture. They escaped and evaded (E and E) for two days through the enemy to Khe Sanh. A very gutsy trip!

Air support for Stiner as he attempted to escape on foot came by way of CPT Ward Britt. CPT Britt spotted the muzzle flashes and made a low-altitude pass over the Automatic Weapon position to drop a smoke grenade. The second fighter in on the position took two hits from the site, but destroyed it with cannon fire. CPT Britt directed continuous fire suppression while a helicopter went in and rescued two crewmembers that lived through the helicopter crash (Howington and one other).

The mélange of fire and smoke and gunfire was taking its toll on all the pilots. From the fourth ship in the formation, CW2 Pullen's account:

We made two or three passes at the LZ but the fire was so heavy, we could get no lower than about 1,000 ft. There was an F-4 that came by low level and dropped the bomb just off our left side. It is still vivid, because I can remember that it seemed so close that you could almost reach out and touch it. I sure would like to know who he was. I believe that is one of the reasons that the rest of us were able to get out without more casualties.

It also seemed to me that most of the NVA thrust was on the lead aircraft and the aircraft in the rear. Major Rex picked up our aircraft 90 degrees to the right and flew down the cliff on the right side of the LZ. I believe if he had done a normal departure that we probably would have taken a lot of hits.

I could see green tracers arching up out of the trees surrounding the LZ being directed at the first three ships in the formation. Soon, it was my turn to fly through the fusillade, and I felt and heard the impact of several .51 caliber projectiles hitting the underside of the helicopter. A single small-caliber round came through my chin bubble and impacted on my chest protector.

When the lead ship carrying LTC Seymoe landed, I was still about 200 feet from touchdown. I saw many olive drab dressed figures emerge from holes in the ground and begin firing on the landing ships.

I decided not to land, and to make a go-around, but since I had a maximum internal load on board, I discovered that I did not have enough power to accomplish this and I had to go to the ground.

At about 50 feet from touchdown, an NVA soldier emerged from a covered hole at my intended landing point, raised an AK-47 to his shoulder, and began firing directly at the nose of the helicopter with full automatic fire ... I can remember the flash of the muzzle and the ejecting brass cases clearly ... The windshield and chin bubbles of the helicopter shattered into pieces ... Instruments popped out of the console and dangled from their connections ... The AK stopped firing as it ran out of ammo, and the NVA soldier turned and ran towards my left into the fire being put down by my left door gunner. He was firing full tracers, and I could see the steady red stream of bullets tearing up the red clay around the soldier's feet ... The NVA reversed his course, and while attempting to duck under the landing helicopter, ran into my left skid at the door position, and I landed on top of him, crushing him with the left skid.

The Marine (Brittingham) was firing at many NVA to my left, who were running towards the ship. One of these soldiers jumped up onto the left skid and grabbed me by my collar through the open side window. I shot him in the face with my sidearm, and he disappeared. After putting the collective control full down, and checking for maximum RPM, I began pulling in pitch to leave the LZ.

I knew then that I still had the cargo on board, and that I might not be able to lift off. I increased collective power until the RPM decreased below 6,000, and pushed the cyclic control forward ... I dragged the helicopter on its skids to the edge of the LZ, and launched it over the side of the hill, nose low to get airspeed as the RPM began to recover.

I passed just to the right of the lead ship, which was upside down, and burning. I didn't see any survivors.

Ahead of me, a gunship making a strafing run, broke off to keep from flying across my path. As I dove into the valley, I gained enough airspeed that the RPM started to increase, and in fact, overspend, so I rolled off on the throttle, realizing that the fuel control was not working, and pulled in more pitch to gain altitude.

As we left the LZ behind, I was getting reports from my gunner, Sp/4 Payne, that one of the ARVN soldiers appeared to be dead, and that the other was wounded and "stapled" to the floor by pieces of the floor paneling.

Payne couldn't get into the left gunner area immediately because of shifted cargo, but soon worked his way over there, and reported that the Marine gunner was seriously wounded, but appeared to be alive.

Since Khe Sanh was the nearest airfield, and I would have to make a running landing, I attempted to turn left to go in that direction, and found that my lateral cyclic controls were severely damaged and that I couldn't do more than shallow left and right turns which were accompanied by severe buffeting.

The fore and aft controls appeared to be OK. My engine and rotor RPM were stable, although being controlled manually by throttle, and my fuel situation was adequate.

I was receiving reports of several aircraft making emergency landings at Khe Sanh, and so I elected to fly directly back to the airfield at La Vang to land, since I could make a running landing there, medical aid was available, and I was pointed in that direction anyway.

Throughout all of this, my pilot, WO Gilmore, was handling the VHF and UHF radios, reporting our position and condition, making arrangements for an ambulance to meet us, and arranging for a replacement aircraft so that we could go back out there and help if needed.

About half way back to Quang Tri, the engine bleed band popped a few times, and stuck open. The engine RPM dropped to 6,000 and the Exhaust Gas Temperature (EGT) rose to the redline. We started to slowly lose altitude. I stayed over the lowest possible elevations, just in case we had to make an emergency landing.

As we neared Quang Tri, I had about 500 feet of altitude, and couldn't see La Vang airfield, off to the right somewhere, and so elected to shoot straight ahead into the Quang Tri compound. There was a schoolyard inside the wire, which was used as a VIP helipad from time to time, but the space was confined, and a running landing wouldn't be possible.

I shot over the minefields, steadily losing altitude, and broke over the fence of the compound into the school yard, to find that it was full of grazing water buffalo, who daintily stepped aside as I put the wounded ship hard on the ground and it came to a stop. As soon as I put the collective control full down, the engine stopped running.

The main rotor system rapidly ground to a stop with the most horrendous grinding and crunching noises. I took off my helmet, unhooked my seat belt and shoulder straps, and my ceramic chest protector broke in half, having been hit three times. Water buffalo scattered as the ambulance and several jeeps raced into the schoolyard.

I went back to check on the young Marine who had been my substitute gunner, and counted ten wounds in his legs, shoulders, and chest area.

His machine gun was littered with silver-gray bullet strikes on the barrel and receiver. His ammo box was empty.

The living ARVN soldier was pinned to the floor, with no other wounds evident on his person, and neither WO Gilmore nor Sp/4 Payne had a mark on them. I had some small cuts on the underside of my chin and jaw from chips of the ceramic material breaking off the chest protector.

As they carried the Marine away on a stretcher, he pulled on my pant leg to get my attention, and said, "You won't need me anymore today, will you sir?"

I told all that I knew about the mission to several people in civilian clothing and military uniforms. We were given something to eat and drink. The Maintenance Officer from Danang brought us another ship, and I got on the radio and contacted LT Ford about what to do. I was instructed to return to Hue Citadel and call it a day, which is what we did. I went to the club in the MACV-SOG compound south of the Perfume River and got drunk.

Once Stiner and Williams were free of the wreckage they decided to run for it. They moved out to the rear, Stiner picking up two grenades and clips for his carbine. Running downhill they encountered a small group of NVA who were so surprised they were able to run right through them. The chase was on when the enemy recovered enough to begin running after them, firing and yelling.

The situation was not good. They had no map, compass, food, water, nor much ammo. The only possibility of survival meant crawling through leech-infested brush and blade-sharp elephant grass, running under cover of darkness with thousands of enemy troops in the area. They weren't likely to get an assist from the combat base. The NVA had scored high that morning with a hit on the ammo dump, killing and wounding many Marines, igniting an inferno that not only blazed for hours, but belched gas and pitched lava-red live rounds into the trenches where Marines were fighting off the initial assaults on the Base's outposts.

After 13 hours of pure terror, Stiner and Williams made Ta Cong hamlet at first light on January 22, where Marine CAC-OSCAR 3's compound was located. They had wandered into a minefield and set one off. Both were now wounded by shrapnel, and Williams was shot by a Marine guard when troops on the line opened up on them, thinking it was the NVA. But their troubles weren't over. The on-edge Marines of CAC-OSCAR 3 thought the two were Russian advisors and took them POW, tying them up overnight. When positive identification was made the Marines apologized, "Sorry 'bout that."

So ended the tragic events of that fatal combat assault. If things had been properly coordinated and planned, if gunships had been allowed to go in and strafe, if Seymoe had either coordinated for artillery fire, or asked Clarke to, the disaster could have been averted. The NVA platoon that waited would not have been successful; however, the desperation and the time of day contributed significantly to what became a disaster.

Others weren't so lucky as Stiner and Williams. Seymoe's body and numerous others were recovered from the site months later by the First Air Cavalry Division. Jerry Elliott's body was not recovered. He is still considered, by his sister, to be an MIA. Her efforts to determine his status are outlined in the Epilogue. Throughout the hearing from which CPT Stiner's comments were taken there was consensus that CW2 McKinsey had been killed and that SSG Billy Hill and Private Jerry Elliott be listed as missing as a result of hostile action.

The 282 Attack Helicopter Company History states: "Two ships landed and crew members tried to help the crew of chalk one, rescuing SP5 David H. Howington. After receiving many hits and one pilot being wounded, the rescue ships were forced to leave the area. Severely damaged ships escaped the LZ and made emergency landings at Khe Sanh and Quang Tri or medevaced wounded to Dong Ha. Tran Dinh Ky, the NVA soldier that shot the helicopter down, was not killed during the battle and because of his actions that day became a National North Vietnamese war hero."

Looking to the north of the French fort into the area behind the pagoda.

Looking to the south of the French fort into the area of the overgrown French minefield.

The front of the pagoda, just to the west of the District Headquarters.

The east side of the pagoda as seen from the back portion of the District Headquarters.

The east side of the pagoda as seen from the District Headquarters trench line.

A major bunker overlooking the pagoda, just to the west of the District Headquarters. (Note the lack of a roof; this picture was taken before the rains of October 1967.)

Bru coming through the wire at FOB 3 to be evacuated.

Bru waiting in the trench line to be evacuated by U.S. Marine Corps helicopters.

Chapter 9

THE BATTLE CONTINUES

The battle for the Khe Sanh District Headquarters lasted almost 24 hours. In spite of the desperate circumstances, the advisory team and the Marines of OSCAR 2 did not yield or concede one square yard of turf to the NVA. Although they started out on defense, because of the effectiveness of the artillery from the Combat Base, the air strikes and their own dogged tenacity, they were soon on the offense, though not outside the wire.

All of the resupply efforts had failed, but during lulls in the action the advisors and Marines were able to redistribute ammunition and reassure their fellow Vietnamese and Bru warriors. Fortunately, throughout the night of January 21, the NVA were unable to make an attack and only sniped. CPT Clarke continually used his "L" shaped artillery concentrations to break up any possible assaults. He marched this artillery all over the area to the south and west of the compound.

CPT Clarke remembers that night as having an eerie, supernatural feel. The day had started fog-bound and filled with rounds of all calibers being fired everywhere. The lulls in the action were few. In contrast the anticipated enemy night attack never materialized. The night was clear and bright thanks to the flickering light from the flares dropped from the Spooky gunship that CPT Clarke had requested. Almost all night long flares were dropped and the enemy had difficulty hiding in the dark. Every time that they were sighted Spooky would engage them with its miniguns.

George Amos describes the night: "That night we burned our classified files and prayed. Luckily, it was very clear that night (no fog) and we had 2 flare planes lighting up the area, we had a B-52 strike and jets guided by radar made bomb runs, and also an old DC-3 with the new gattling guns (fires 4000 rounds a second) flew overhead. It is called 'SPOOKY' because those guns are weird sounding—just like a buzz saw. We had a radio in our bunker that was connected to the communications bunker and we knew that if the radio quit broadcasting it was all over. Through the nite we kept receiving sporadic sniper fire and mortar rounds. But they did not attack in force."

CPT Clarke used all avenues available to request an ARC Light. An ARC Light is a B-52 strike. Three bombers in formation drop bombs resulting in a saturation bombing of an area approximately 1 kilometer wide and 3 kilometers long. Based upon CPT Nhi's monitoring of NVA nets and an evaluation of where the NVA would go for another assault, the ARC Light was requested. In the middle of the night a B-52 mission went in south of the District Compound in the area that CPT Clarke had recommended to Bob Brewer. They had guessed where the NVA were going to be and they got them. This resulted in the destruction of the remnants of a regiment, according to a Chieu–hoi (NVA or VC who voluntarily surrendered) that turned up at Lang Vei several days later. He reported that his regiment had been decimated twice—the first time as they came down the Ho Chi Minh Trail and the second time in the attacks against the District Headquarters and the subsequent air strikes on its positions. After the first ARC Light decimation the unit returned to North Vietnam for refitting. The Chieu-hoi was not interested in doing that again. He had had enough.

That night Bob Brewer told CPT Clarke to consider surrendering if things got too tough. CPT Clarke resolved not to surrender and never shared this discussion with the rest of his advisory team.

The Marines from CAP 2 came into the compound in small teams of two to four, during the early morning hours when it was still dark. They had been out of communications and did not know what to expect when they busted out of their compound and charged toward the District Compound. They made this 250- to 350-meter run with great fear. Corpsman Roberts Remembers:

> We didn't know what to think—if we would be gunned down leaving the compound or what. We were nearly out of ammo and had no idea what lay in store for us.

Sergeant Balanco opened the gate each time and then positioned them where he needed them. They were happy to be reunited with their fellow

Marines and the defenders in the compound. Corpsman Roberts remembers this escape from OSCAR 2 as follows:

> That night, however, it seemed hopeless! SGT Harper told us we had three options: slip out through the wire under cover of night and make our way in two- man teams back to the base, surrender and become POWs, or defend our positions and fight to the death. We all voted for option number 3, and prepared to meet our fate, ready to make the enemy's victory as costly as possible.
>
> Throughout the night, we redistributed ammunition, filled our canteens, licked our wounds, and said a few prayers. We knew that if there were to be a withdrawal, we would be left out in the cold unless we were able to join up right now with the CAC-1 at the District Headquarters. Our assumption was correct.
>
> Radio communications were poor at best and we were in the dark about what was happening at the Combat Base, the hill units stationed on the strategic hill-tops around the Combat Base, and our own brother CAP units.
>
> The distance between the two CAP units was about 350 meters and the NVA had been entrenched around both compounds. We decided to break out and attack the enemy wherever we found him. SGT Harper instructed me to patch up the wounded as best I could. I used the last of my morphine on those in the most pain and paired up the strongest with the weakest. We decided to either live or die together. We were determined not to lose a single Marine or Bru.
>
> We sent out our two fastest men to recon by fire and break through enemy lines. Three minutes later we all charged! Talk about getting pumped! We ran shooting, shouting, and screaming AROOGAH!!
>
> The guys at OSCAR 1 couldn't believe what we had done, and admitted to us that they had just about written us off. Some even thought we had already gotten wiped out. They were certainly glad for the reinforcement, as they too were in a pickle.

Jim Perry remembers the night of January 21 as being quiet, but busy. He recounts:

> Over the next 24 hours I heard all sorts of screams, yelling, calls for help etc. from our own compound. A 105 round fell short (Marine supporting fire from the base) and landed in a short trench line killing two Bru PFs. The short trench line was to the extreme left side of the frontal area of our compound as you came in the gate, very near a local building. I rushed out but they were dead. I knew that if I left them there they would spook the rest of the PFs (they were all easily spooked—Bru and Vietnamese alike,

believed they saw ghosts, etc.). I carried them to the east side of the HQ building and covered them until more definitive measures could be made to get the bodies off the compound. More Bru were to follow them. I had several wounded in the Headquarters building. I knew I had to get them out of the building before the NVA tried to B-40 it to death or our own 105 support might unintentionally level it. I moved several into CPT Nhi's bunker so their own medic could watch them–they were already stabilized. There was little room in the MACV bunker with barely room to fart. I made two trips back to the RF compound (French Fort) during the night of the 21st. They had some real bleeding problems back there and the RF medics were having problems starting IV's because of partially collapsed circulatory systems of some of the wounded RFs. We got them stabilized and they were placed in bunkers, not in some of those western town shanties they had on the compound back there.

SFC Perry's matter-of-fact description is indicative of the courage and bravery that he exhibited to aid the compound's warriors. That night SFC Kasper of the advisory team put a bottle of scotch in one of the leg pockets of his jungle fatigue uniform and bourbon in the other. CPT Clarke remembers him coming back to the command bunker and asking which pocket he wanted. CPT Clarke demurred as he needed all of his wits about him.

The next morning was clear and bright and the area was clear of the enemy. There were several patrols mounted to sweep the area. The initial focus was on the area immediately to the south of the compound and the village itself. The NVA had backed off. There were hundreds of bodies, numerous blood trails and over 100 weapons, including the first RPG-7 and AK-74 found in South Vietnam. Some of these still had Cosmoline on them.

Jim Perry remembers:

The morning of 22 January dawned clear and bright with no enemy to be found anywhere. Captain Clarke and SFC Kasper took a small patrol to the west and south of the compound and found numerous bodies and weapons. SFC King went to the police station and towards the bridge on the east end of the village. The people were starting to come out of their homes and bunkers and many were already walking towards the Combat Base.

George Amos:

The next morning when the sun came up we knew we would make it. We had lasted the night! You can not believe how we felt. All I did was think about you, love and home. I also did *much praying*. It's a terrible feeling sitting in a bunker for 30 hours and not expecting to live. We thought all hope had been lost. But at 10:30 Monday morning, the enemy withdrew, I guess to regroup and we got out. Jim and I got the last helicopter that was able to land before the mortar attack started again. As soon as we could after the attack Jim and I left the compound: first we went down into the village to look for our Vietnamese counterparts. They were gone and I figure they were killed. We were greeted by the villagers like heroes. It was great! There were enemy bodies all around the perimeter of our little camp. I counted 40 bodies (*and got 2 rolls of pictures.*) plus much equipment and parts of bodies. There was a hand and arm hanging on the barbed wire (took pictures).

At this time everyone was exhilarated by the great victory that had been won. The CAC, Bru, and RF Company were picking up weapons. Over 100 weapons were recovered and stored in the RF compound. Early in this process a Marine helicopter landed to take LT Stamper to the Combat Base to meet with COL Lounds. He was never to return.

SGT Balanco took approximately four Marines and at least eight Bru, who were all volunteers, and patrolled down the road toward the Old French Fort, which sat on a hill just to the south of Route 9. They were still very nervous and disturbed at the death and destruction they had so recently experienced at the Ville. The memory of the bloodshed and destruction weighed heavily on them, but they continued on. They made it to the bottom of the hill and came in view of three or four uniformed soldiers up on a bunker. SGT Balanco thought they might be Vietnamese soldiers from the 256th RF Company, but CPL Russell questioned that conclusion due to the fact that they were too far off to see their uniforms clearly. Balanco and Russell waved and yelled at the soldiers to come down, but the unidentified soldiers seemed unimpressed with the request and waved back, and without speaking motioned for the newcomers to come up to the bunker. Balanco found this to be very unsettling and, being highly suspicious, he took the patrol back to the compound at Khe Sanh Ville. He felt sure they were NVA. But to this day it is not known if they were survivors of the previous day's ambush or NVA trying to entice the patrol into an ambush. The latter is probably the case.

A few of the CAP Marines searched and hunted for souvenirs from the slaughtered NVA. They reported that they saw hundreds of mutilated and mangled NVA just on the west side of the compound near the pagoda. The emotional reaction of these Marines was one of elation—they had the won the battle and survived. To them went the spoils of the battle. They gathered rifles, RPG-weapons, and personal military gear from the bodies. Many of the AK-47s and AK-44s were brand new, some with Cosmoline on them. CPT Nhi notes that, "Many NVA bodies and their fully loaded weapons, including RPG-7s were recovered along the warehouse wall beneath the bunker." The various patrols gathered the first RPG-7s ever seen in Vietnam and more than 150 weapons which were taken and stored in the RF storage area in the French Fort.

Some of the Marines still have many souvenirs including belts, packs, knives, canteens, entrenching tools, money, ammo pouches, rifle cleaning gear, etc. The most prized of the war trophies was an officer's belt buckle with a red star on it.

In addition to the trophies several of these Marines took back something that was to change their lives forever. They came to appreciate that the cost of losing was life itself. This haunts them to this day.

George Amos's final thoughts on the day reflect what many of us felt:

Not all got out, but we were lucky. Any way, all I got out with me was my one uniform, a steel helmet, a pistol and an M-16. I'll have to get new clothes. I don't know what happened to the others. The news says nothing about it. All I know is that I was very lucky. The other two camps in the area were hit again and overrun when the US troops ran out of ammo. A Sergeant saved my life. I was looking out the bunker window when a mortar round hit. The Sergeant was standing behind me and took the shrapnel. If he hadn't been there, it would have hit me in the face. As it was it hit the sergeant in the back of the head—not *too* badly.

Any way, we got out and now I am *safely* in Danang, VN. *Not a scratch!!* But *I'm still shaking, and very happy to be alive.* It was the second nicest anniversary present I could think of. The best would be to home with you. From now on—*NO MORE VOLUNTEERING!!!*

I know what war is really like and I know what it feels like to think that you have only a few hours to live, and I tell you, that I appreciate life much, much more. From now on no dangerous assignments. I will not go back because our operation was 'blown' and all our records destroyed. *NO SWEAT!!!!*

It's all over, so don't worry!!!! And by the way—*HAPPY ANNIVERSARY*—2 wonderful years.

How's the baby? and *you* dear. I love you. I'm out of paper so goodnite love. I love you.

PS: I'll probably get a bunch of medals for this

PPS: anything else on the news about Khe Sanh isn't true.

LT Stamper later told the CAP Marines that the forward air controller (FAC) estimated as many as one thousand NVA were killed or wounded in the area surrounding the compound at Khe Sanh Ville.

Against all odds the small force of Vietnamese, Bru, Marines, and Army advisors had done what no one probably expected that they could do—they had fought and won. The attacking NVA force had been decimated. The combination of individual bravery, well-orchestrated artillery, and air strikes had been effective, but the exhilaration that was to come from this victory was short lived, as the larger game plan required that the obstacles to the large-scale use of firepower had to be removed. The valiant garrison had to be withdrawn.

Total casualties in the defending force were five Bru and six RFs killed—the RFs were all in the triangular shaped fort at the back of the compound where the brunt of the attack came. The company commander was one of those killed. The RF Company had the 60 mm mortar and CPT Nhi coordinated fire with them.

How did this small force of 175 Bru Montagnards, Vietnamese soldiers, Army advisors, Marines, and a Navy Corpsman get themselves into this isolated situation? They were placed in this position by the overall strategic plan, to which they were not privy. They nevertheless fought the most successful ground battle of the entire 77-day siege, destroying an NVA regiment, a fact verified by a captured NVA soldier. How was this small band of disparate warriors able to render a North Vietnamese regiment of over 2,000 soldiers combat ineffective? By personal valor and well-orchestrated firepower. This having been said, further elaboration on these themes would be useful.

WHAT COULD HAVE BEEN DONE DIFFERENTLY

In reflecting upon the battle for the village, numerous things come to mind that might have improved the effectiveness of the forces in the village. Eleven killed and 29 wounded is a high price and this does not include the losses from the failed heliborne relief operation. However, there is every indication that the combined efforts of CAC-OSCAR 1 and 2, the District Forces and air and artillery rendered an NVA regiment combat ineffective.

By considering the NVA after-action comments at Appendix 7, one comes away with a better appreciation of what did and didn't happen. The NVA acknowledge the death of the 7th Battalion Commander. The weapons captured and the bodies seen by both the defenders and the FACs suggest that there was a regiment, not a battalion involved in the attack. Why would a Front-level set of graphics, as shown on the map overlay in Appendix 4 show an axis for companies? (A direction of attack arrow on a military map.) That is not normally how graphical depictions are done. The data suggest the involvement of all three battalions of the 66th Regiment, not just the 7th Battalion.

It is also interesting to note that the NVA acknowledge a hard fight and that it took them 24 hours to gain control of the District Headquarters. One can only guess that the initial success that they refer to is the forces that were in the area near the police station.

From what one reads in the NVA description in Appendix 4, it is obvious that the District Forces were successful and that the NVA suffered heavy causalities, but what could have been done better?

There is an inherent dilemma for any advisory team. They are advisors, not commanders. They can suggest, advise, and assist. Potentially, the advisors become more powerful based upon their ability to acquire and orchestrate fire support and other assets.

The District Headquarters' basic defense plan worked, but there are several things that would have made the defense better.

CAC-OSCAR 2

The CAC-OSCAR should have been required to have an integrated communications plan. The absence of information as to what was happening just down the road made it harder to understand the big picture. It also made it difficult to integrate fire support. The best thing that could have been done was to bury wire between OSCAR 2 and the command bunker.

Facilities

In retrospect the District Forces might have been better off to have included the pagoda to the west of the actual compound as part of the compound. By placing the pagoda into the defensive perimeter of the District Headquarters, the District Forces could have denied the enemy a significant fighting position. Additional listening posts outside of the wire might have provided more early warning. It might have also been a good idea to have started the efforts at clearing fields of fire sooner. More cleared space between the defenders and the attackers would have allowed for longer range fire to have been placed on the enemy.

CPT Nhi did give considerable thought to the weaknesses of the District Compound defense caused by the locations of the AID warehouse and the Pagoda. There was no permanent bunker built on top of the AID warehouse. The logic was that the enemy reconnaissance would see it and would destroy it before launching an assault. However, he did place a bunker on top of the warehouse, which was to have a dramatic impact on the battle, as noted.

CPT Nhi agrees as to the desirability of placing the Pagoda inside the defensive perimeter. Unfortunately for political reason no District Chief would have wanted to do so. However, I did have a plan to solve this problem in my artillery support plan. The plan existed when a platoon of 105mm located at Lang Vei base with an ARVN battalion. If the enemy used the Pagoda as a cover to launch an assault to the District Compound, I wouldn't hesitate in one second to use artillery to destroy the building. I kept this delicate decision for myself. If it was leaked out, I would be in trouble with the Buddhists.

Because of Nhi's forethought in strengthening the bunkers, not one of them on the defensive perimeter was destroyed by the NVA. He notes that, "The NVA didn't have a chance to use their RPG-7s or they were not effective, nor were their B-40's able to destroy the bunkers. B-40 rounds hit the PSP and exploded and the red clay absorbed the shock."

Plans

Actual plans for the heliborne relief should have been developed. In fact, we should have developed multiple contingency plans, rather than trust to only the Marines. We could have asked the Special Forces at Lang Vei to also come to our assistance. If there had been unity of command, so that the myriad of units in the area were working together in a synchronized manner, planning would have been much better. Better fire-support plans for the combined defense of CAC-OSCAR 2 and the District Headquarters would also have made sense. Fire-support plans should have been built for each of the relief operations. This might have helped the combat assault significantly—especially if everyone knew that such plans existed. Finally, a breakout plan to escape to the combat base would have made everyone involved more comfortable.

Rehearsals

Months earlier the Marines ran a half-hearted rehearsal of the relief of the District Headquarters. As the situation began to change and more forces came into the area, we should have rehearsed the Marine relief several more times. We should have also rehearsed with LTC Seymoe or someone at the province level the heliborne operation—at least the air battle captain should have worked his way through the sequence of events, the use of supporting arms, etc. With each plan that was developed we should have had a rehearsal so that everyone knew what was expected of them.

Leadership

The Vietnamese military has received some undeserved caustic remarks about the leadership of its officers. Earlier CPT Nhi described what he had done to earn the trust and confidence of both the people and the soldiers whom he was charged with leading. The results of the battle illustrate clearly the pay off. CPT Nhi continues:

As we all knew, Lt. LY the Company commander was killed within 20 minutes of the attack, yet all the RFs remained calm and fought vigorously. It was not an ordinary occurrence in such a circumstance. I told the platoon leaders and the staff sergeant of the company that I took command of the company; they reported directly to me. Having trust in me made the difference. Having said that, I never forget the presence of 3 brave Marines at the RF's defense quarter; their bravery definitely lifted the RF's morale.

In this remote mountain district, the people (soldiers, cadres and civilians could easily find out under what circumstance the chief was assigned to the post). They would measure the integrity and mettle of an officer by watching his devotion to the job. I neither complained nor asked Quang Tri for anything. I didn't have a jeep for transportation as other District Chiefs had. That was ok! As long as Quang Tri took care of sending enough rice for the civilians, I was satisfied. Due to the unique situation in Khe Sanh, I felt that my presence was more important to the peace of mind of everyone in Khe Sanh. I was summoned to Quang Tri for provincial meetings every few months. I left in the morning and returned at noontime the next day. I was supposed to get 10 days off (vacation) so that I could visit my parents living in Saigon. In 1967, I skipped my vacation so that I could be with my troops all the time. My efforts in building trust and serving people well paid off during the battle.

CPT Nhi highlights one of the most critical aspects of leadership—trust. When CPT Clarke and SFC King walked out of Khe Sanh with the District Forces, they not only displayed their trust of those that they accompanied, but they also earned the trust of those brave men.

The battlefield bravery and leadership of SGT Balanco and many of the Marines was also significant in securing the hard-fought victory.

Focus and Unity of Effort

CPT Clarke should have accelerated his efforts to build a coherent team within the compound and with the other elements within the district. This would have lead to better teamwork among all of the disparate units. This is a mission that should have fallen to COL Lounds, as the senior man on the ground. Someone should have accomplished this mission. What one had in Khe Sanh was a microcosm of what existed throughout I Corps—multiple, not necessarily focused, activities—no unity of command and effort.

Patrols

When the morning of January 22 came and the enemy was gone, there was no plan for securing the area and searching for all of the bodies and equipment. There also was no plan for repairing the defenses and getting back to work on the basic mission of providing security for the local population. LTC Corson in the earlier quote highlights that after defeating the

NVA was the time to pursue building improved relations with the local inhabitants. We did not think of that.

In essence the District Team had not thought through all of the implications of a major attack. Was this a unique situation, or was it the nature of the defensive, attrition-oriented strategy that was being conducted in the war? Was it a result of not anticipating a major assault of the scope that was experienced? Was it a result of the peaceful nature of the 6 months prior to this attack? The answer is probably all of the above.

THE EVACUATION OF THE DISTRICT HEADQUARTERS

In spite of their victory, COL Lounds, CO, 26th Marine Regiment, ordered the evacuation of CAC-OSCAR from the compound. He told CPT Clarke by radio that he could no longer support the District Compound with artillery fire. Without the Marines and their artillery support CPT Clarke did not know how he could defend the District Headquarters. This was reported to Quang Tri and the agonizing decision was made there to evacuate the District Headquarters. The Marines and the wounded were evacuated by air. The Vietnamese civilians from the village walked to the Combat Base. Over 1,000 Vietnamese showed up at the Combat Base that day and the next and were evacuated by air to the coast. One of them, whose face epitomizes the agony that was Khe Sanh, had her picture on the cover of many national publications. She was the woman who did the advisors' laundry and each day baked fresh bread for them. (The picture is in the Appendix 3)

CPT Clarke and SFC King led the District Headquarters forces on what seemed to be an interminable trek, bypassing Hill 471 to bring the forces to the safety of FOB-3, which was attached to the Khe Sanh Combat Base. They were met there with food, water, medical support, and a loud, "Well done."

Bob Brewer notes that:

> General Troung, of the 1st ARVN Division, was totally opposed to this course of action (evacuating the District Headquarters). His point of view was that this would be the first Government of Vietnam political seat to be lost to the Communists, and it shouldn't happen without a fight. CPT Clarke's point was that the Marines were not prepared to fight for the place, and he was not prepared to lose his team in an unsupported outpost.

Bob Brewer closed the chapter on the fight for the village and the District Headquarters when he said:

> The Communists were ecstatic about capturing their *first* political headquarters. They went bananas over this, and my Government of Vietnam

counterparts could not understand why the American military was so unconcerned. What we should have done was go right back in immediately and retake Huong Hoa District Headquarters. But by then, our military leaders had embraced the idea of the "set piece battle," which they expected to win.

He did not know that the Special Forces had offered a Mike Force (a heavily armed company-sized force led by Special Forces) to retake the compound or that GEN Westmoreland had made the decision at least by early January to attempt to engage the NVA in a battle at Khe Sanh.

CPT Nhi notes that, "The 37th ARVN Ranger battalion was flown into Khe Sanh with the intention of retaking the District Headquarters. The decision was made by LTG Hoang Xuan Lam. I Corps Commander at the time. The battalion commander was a Dalat classmate of mine." However, at some point this intent was countermanded and the battalion spent the siege defending the most critical avenue of approach into the Combat Base.

The events of January 21–22 were an emotional roller coaster for the participants. They went from the fear and adrenalin of the foggy morning fight, to the concern over relief and resupply, to the agony of feeling abandoned, to the ecstasy of the clear morning light and realization that the fight had been won, to the final low of abandoning the District Headquarters and giving away to the North Vietnamese what they couldn't win by force of arms.

On January 31, 1968, CPT Clarke wrote home:

As you have probably figured out, there has been a large battle here in Khe Sanh. At 0500 on the 21st 3 battalions of NVA attacked the District Headquarters where I was. We fought all day and night and then had to evacuate the afternoon of the 22nd. We estimate that we killed about 600 NVA while having 6 Vietnamese and 5 Bru killed and 28 wounded. When we evacuated I left everything behind except my .45 pistol, my M-16, a PRC-25 radio and my ammunition. We went to Khe Sanh Combat Base where we have been incorporated into a defensive perimeter. All we've been doing now is waiting for the big attack and "digging in." I am like a battalion commander. I command 375 indigenous troops and 28 Americans.

Chapter 10

THE ADVISORY TEAM ON THE MOVE

Throughout the trek from the District Headquarters CPT Clarke continually consulted with CPT Nhi who was coordinating the local security of the little band. He also used the PRC-25 radio that he was carrying to periodically update the Province Advisory Headquarters through the radio relay. He also arranged for their reception and insured that supporting fires would be available, if necessary through FOB-3. Together the two captains continued to complement each other's activities.

The Marine leadership would not allow armed Vietnamese or Bru inside of the Combat Base. Westmoreland stated in his memoirs that this action was justified because of the fear that the "mob" had been infiltrated by enemy agents. Taken at face value this is probably a valid concern. However, it is just part of a bigger theme that runs throughout this period of history. The Marine leadership at the Combat Base was never comfortable with its armed allies. There was nowhere for armed District Forces to go into but FOB-3, an appendage of the combat base. The band made it to FOB-3 safely, where they were welcomed and their needs taken care of. They were quickly integrated into the defense of the perimeter.

On the afternoon of their arrival CPT Clarke was part of a Special Forces strike team led by MAJ Simcox of FOB-3 that conducted a heliborne raid back into the District Headquarters to destroy everything that the District Forces had left behind and to evacuate the over 150 weapons that the District Forces had captured. Included in these weapons were the first RPG-7s recovered in South Vietnam. The force mistakenly flew into an LZ south of the normal compound LZ , one helicopter at a time, and CPT Clarke then led the way through the old French minefield to enter the compound. The raiding party was broken into three teams. One team went for the weapons in the RF compound (French Fort) where they had been stored, the second went into the advisor's area led by CPT Clarke and the third set the explosives in the warehouse and checked out the east end of the compound. The weapons were hauled to the regular LZ, loaded on the helicopters, and evacuated as the raiding party continued to go through the compound. In addition to evacuating the weapons, many of the other usable supplies were rigged for destruction. CPT Clarke put thermite grenades into all of the advisors' records and left grenades with the pins pulled between soda, food, and beer cans both in the refrigerator and on the storage shelves. In all he left about ten grenades as booby traps. As the force was departing the compound the NVA were marching in the front gate on the north. Laying on the floor of the last Huey out CPT Clarke emptied his 30-round magazine at the NVA force.

The fact that the NVA were just approaching the compound late on the afternoon of January 22 suggests that they had not expected the District Headquarters to be evacuated and may not have been ready to occupy it. Several days later, a patrol going into the village also suggests that only a small NVA force was in the vicinity. COL Lounds's request for a subsequent patrol back into the District Headquarters on the January 26, may have been prompted by the limited forces noted in the area on the January 22.

That night CPTs Clarke and Nhi had the opportunity to listen to tapes that the FOB-3 personnel had recorded of the activity on the enemy radio nets during the critical parts of the battle. They agreed that they had always had a fairly clear picture of what was going on, though they did not know that the ambush of the heliborne relief force was coming. The question was never asked of why the information from the monitoring effort had not been shared with the District Headquarters defenders at the time. It would have helped. The obvious answer was that secure communications were not available and no one wanted to compromise what they were listening to on the NVA nets. This is a recurring theme throughout this effort—not wanting to compromise intelligence sources and methods.

Also that night, after the raid, the two captains listened to the NVA command nets and heard them discussing the booby traps exploding in the Headquarters building and the NVA efforts at trying to start and use the abandoned truck and jeep in front of the District Headquarters. Then, working with their previous preplanned artillery plots, the two coordinated with the Combat Base Fire Direction Center for a time-on-target artillery fire mission, nothing more was heard from that radio station.

On January 24, 1968, CPT Clarke wrote his parents:

No matter what you read in the papers I'm all right as is all of my team. One of them was lightly wounded. Say a few prayers for us. Charlie got everything that I had over here so if your address was among them Charlie may write you so just don't pay attention to what he says.

During the next 2 weeks following the evacuation of the District Headquarters both sides consolidated their positions. The perimeter at the Combat Base was being reinforced, supplies and additional troops were being added, and very little, if anything, was being done for the local population. On the North Vietnamese side the same was true. They began to slowly invest the Combat Base by moving troops into the area under cover of darkness. They were positioning their long-range artillery that would be used in subsequent phases. They were also securing their lines of communications.

The district government, forces, and advisors spent the next $2^1/_2$ months in exile at the FOB-3 part of the Khe Sanh Combat Base where they dodged artillery rounds, took part in the defense of the Combat Base, and operated an intelligence net. They thought of themselves as a government in exile. The next $2^1/_2$ months saw the fall of the Lang Vei Special Forces Camps, the 77-day siege of the Combat Base, and then Operation PEGASUS, which was the relief operation conducted by the 1st Cavalry Division.

The period after the abandonment of the District Headquarters was one of consolidation at FOB-3 for the entire complement that had left the village. CPT Clarke continued to work with CPT Nhi and his "government in exile." The RFs were sent back to Quang Tri to refit, while the CAC-O Marines with their PFs volunteered to become part of the defensive perimeter of FOB-3, and stayed until April 7, 1968. The Bru PFs were glad to be back together with their Marines.

LANG VEI FALLS

The 33rd Royal Laotian Infantry Battalion and the Special Forces at Lang Vei were threats to the NVA lines of communications. For this reason in early February the NVA attacked the 33rd. In this attack in Laos they used PT-76 light amphibious tanks. The 33rd was quickly overrun and retreated into South Vietnam. They were received, cared for, and rearmed by the Special Forces at Lang Vei, who set them up in the old camp, which had been overrun the spring before, with their own team of Special Forces advisors. FOB-3 with its resources and past ties with the 33rd Royal Laotian Battalion assisted in this effort.

The men at Lang Vei had not wasted their time during the lull. They had further enhanced their own defenses. The reports of the NVA using tanks against the 33rd Royal Laotians were taken seriously by the Special

Forces. They tried to obtain antitank mines from the Marines to reinforce their defenses, but their requests were denied. They increased the number of soldiers deployed to defend the two camps.

During this time the strategic situation was taking a dramatic turn. The Tet Offensive of 1968 started at the end of the month. The strategic focus was diverted from the Combat Base to the streets of Saigon. Tet was turning into a military defeat for the NVA. The VC units were decimated, the main force units were badly mauled, and the people did not rise up to support the invaders. However, the U.S. public had exceeded its tolerance of the war. Along with the news of Khe Sanh, televisions and newspapers carried the picture of the police chief in Cholon shooting a "suspected" VC. The graphic photo enflamed a public already disillusioned with the seemingly unwinnable war. In Washington, the Tet Offensive promoted debates about the direction and wisdom of the war and President Johnson decided to bow out of the 1968 presidential election. He called for the cessation of bombing of North Vietnam and began seeking peace talks with Hanoi. He grudgingly accepted Westmoreland's request for an additional 206,000 troops and soon after he replaced Westmoreland with GEN Creighton Abrams. U.S. policymakers needed to find a way to deescalate the war in Vietnam.

Against the backdrop of the Tet Offensive, which began at the end of January, and with attention therefore riveted elsewhere, the NVA attacked Lang Vei in the middle of the night of February 7 using PT-76 tanks. During the defense there were many heroic actions by U.S. and Vietnamese defenders but when first light came there were NVA tanks sitting on top of the Special Forces command bunker and the occupants of the old camp were under attack. As in the case of Khe Sanh village, the Marine leadership at the Combat Base were asked to execute their contingency relief mission but refused. They were then asked to conduct a helicopter evacuation and again refused. The Special Forces at FOB-3 were preparing their own relief action and trying to gather the helicopters to make it possible. They were supporting the effort in every way they could. This illustrates that the FOB-3 Special Forces were loyal to their comrades and did not feel restrained or under the control of COL Lounds and the 26th Marines.

Lang Vei provides another example of a force being expendable—at least from the Marine leadership's perspective and probably also from Westmoreland's perspective. The camp had been reinforced and efforts were made to defend it. If the goal was a set-piece battle around Khe Sanh Combat Base, Lang Vei was also part of the bait to draw the NVA in. Evacuating the camp would have tipped the intent.

There is a historical controversy at this point—the issue of evacuation helicopters. GEN Westmoreland reports that he ordered the Marines to provide helicopters to evacuate the Americans from the camps. However, COL Ladd, the 5th Special Forces Commander, reports that he had diffi- culty getting in to see GEN Westmoreland and turned to GEN Abrams to make a decision. He reports that GEN Abrams immediately called the 3rd Marine Division Air Commander and told him to execute the evacuation mission.

The missions were flown and the brave U.S. Army defenders of the camp and the Vietnamese and Laotian leadership were evacuated. The remainder of the force and the civilians (Bru and Laotian) that were in the area were left to their own devices. Most of them chose to trek cross-country to the Combat Base. When this mob arrived several days later, they were disarmed by the Marines and turned away. This group of Bru, Laotian, and Vietnamese soldiers and Montagnard civilians then trekked cross-country to Cam Lo, some 45 unfriendly kilometers away along Highway 9 to the east. CPT Clarke alerted Quang Tri that the refugees were coming and food, clothing, and medical care were awaiting them when they got to Cam Lo.

After the NVA attack supported by tanks on Lang Vei, the armor threat to the Combat Base was taken much more seriously. Antitank mines were made available and were emplaced, the few Marine antitank weapons (a platoon of tanks and some lightly armored vehicles each mounting six 106 mm recoilless rifles) were repositioned and some thought given to using their mobility. CPT Clarke, as an Armor officer, was consulted as to the best use of these assets. He recommended the formation of mobile reaction teams held in a central reserve. [He remembered his studies of St. Vith in the Battle of the Bulge and how Brigadier General (BG) Bruce C. Clarke (no relation) had been successful in countering every German attack using such forces.]

Following the fall of Lang Vei the stage was set for an extended siege. The "agony of Khe Sanh" had truly begun. Day in and day out the Combat Base was subjected to artillery, mortar, and rocket fire. The fire was the most intense when aircraft were landing to deliver supplies or pick up people. The rounds would literally follow the aircraft up and down the runway. Several were hit. It became so difficult for aircraft that most supplies were delivered by airdrop or resupply helicopters. High-priority items were delivered using Low Altitude Parachute Extraction System (LAPES). LAPES required the aircraft to roll down the runway and have a pallet pulled out of the aircraft using a parachute.

LIFE AT FOB-3

The occupants of FOB-3 felt segregated and isolated. The Americans were not allowed on the base with their fighting Bru or Cambodians. COL Lounds did not want any armed native troops on the Khe Sanh Combat Base. The 37th ARVN Ranger Battalion was flown in and immediately dug in outside the Marine's wire near the airstrip. A short distance from FOB-3 were several Marine tanks with their turrets turned and their guns pointed directly at the warriors of FOB-3. If that was not enough, *Cambodian mercenaries* were entrenched right behind the PFs and CAC Marines on the southern part of the FOB-3 perimeter. They were being paid by SOG personnel to guard the "million dollar bunker" (the nickname given by the Marines to the bunker built to house the SOG Special Forces soldiers, their aid station, and operations areas).

A CORPSMAN'S PERSPECTIVE

John Roberts has a slightly different story to tell:

The Marine Combat Base at Khe Sanh was not much of a fortress, as the press would later describe it. When we, the Marine CAC, along with the South Vietnamese Officials of the District Headquarters arrived via our helicopter rescue from Khe Sanh Village, we were pretty beat up and tired. There was little time to relax or ease the stress of our ordeal.

We were immediately placed with the U.S. Army Forward Operating Base 3 on the edge of the Marine Combat Base and were under the command and control of the Army Special Forces rather than Marine commanders. For some, this was unacceptable, but I thought we had lucked out.

The Army had better communications with the outside world, better logistical support, better small arms, and seemed to have a slightly different view of what this war was all about.

The Siege was to last some 77 days, and during that period of time there was never a day without some combat, some casualties, killed or wounded in action. Politics was the least of our worries.

The sense of the Marines was one of survival, and there was a built-in instinct that demanded action. They kept asking the unit commanders, when are we going to go on the offensive and give those bastards some of their own medicine? It seems that it is not natural for Marines to allow the enemy the initiative. They were barely able to obey their orders to wait, wait, and wait some more for the enemy to come to us. It is their nature to patrol aggressively and engage the enemy wherever they find him.

What the Marines at all levels of command and control did not share with the front-line units was the bigger picture, the tactics and the politics of the fight for Khe Sanh. Did it really matter at the time? In retrospect, yes it did! After 28 years, yes it still does!

John Roberts continues:

Another major concern of the medical staff was that after a few days, we began to have a massive rat infestation. This was a direct result of troopers throwing open C-ration containers out in front of their fighting positions and later the presence of the dead NVA assault forces, which ended up being partially consumed by the rats. These rats were not like the ones you see in New York or the fields of West Texas. These rats were gigantic! Some estimated them to weigh as much as 12–15 pounds and they were aggressive as hell!

Many of the troops of the line were bitten while they catnapped in between skirmishes. This resulted in medical evacuations for some that may have been exposed to rabies. Later, too many were bitten and could not realistically be relieved and evacuated. The decision was made that the medical personnel would simply have to instruct the troops themselves or their buddies in the proper procedures to give injections daily in their stomachs to ward off rabies. In spite of the bites, we were unable to confirm a single verified case of rabies.

Bob Donoghue, one the SOG Special Forces soldiers, remembers that:

Khe Sanh's rats lived in the sandbagged bunkers off the remains of food found in C-ration cans. As nighttime approached they would emerge from their nests to scurry about the area. Anyone trying to get some sleep at one time or another had one of these critters run across their body. During this time period several people were bitten and had to undergo an extremely painful series of rabies shots.

The tide slowly turned against these rats due to the deteriorating weather conditions and the North Vietnamese Army. The only way to supply the troops with food and ammunition was by parachute drops. After several days of heavy enemy fire and lousy flying weather, the resupply drops tapered off creating a shortage of rations.

Our indigenous troops, the Bru Montagnards, soon devised a plan to supplement their meager rations. First, they would take a small individual equipment net and stretch it across the bottom half of a trench. They would have two other men start beating on the bunker sandbags with pieces of 2 × 4's. The rats, startled by the banging, would scurry out the bunker and down the trench line only to be entangled within the net. A short time later the Bru would be heating up water in a #10 can with pieces of C-4 explosive and throwing the rats into the can to cook them. These Khe Sanh rodents provided fine dining at a time when rations were limited. As the siege progressed it became harder and harder for the Bru to find these fine tasting rodents.

THE NORTHERN HALF OF FOB-3

On the northern end of the FOB-3 compound, life was much different. The northern end of the compound was directly in front of the Base's 155-mm howitzer battery. These guns were a prime target for the NVA rockets and artillery. It was also the highest point in the compound and thus provided excellent observation. CPT Clarke and three Special Forces sergeants occupied the northern corner bunker. CPT Nhi had a bunker nearby.

During this period the roles were reversed. CPT Clarke commanded the northern half of the compound and was responsible for developing fields of fire, living bunkers, and fighting positions. CPT Nhi helped him by dealing with the PFs. Communications trenches were dug from the defensive trench lines to the command bunker and dug-in latrines. The living bunkers were on the back of the trench line and defensive/fighting positions were on the front. Following the first probe additional cover was added to the back of the trench lines and to cover the entrances to the fighting positions because during that probe Marines to their rear had opened fire and the biggest threat came from them. The southern sector of the compound had Cambodians hired by SOG behind the CAC defenders. In the northern part of the sector there were Marines 75 meters behind the defenders and there were not any routes through their wire and they did open fire during a probe. Between the base and the defenders of FOB-3 on the north was a strip of tangle-foot, concertina wire, and landmines, segregating the men of FOB-3 with their indigenous troops from the Marines at Khe Sanh Combat Base. If attacked they had nowhere to go.

This valuable piece of real estate was further protected by machine guns and recoilless rifles manned by Marines and aimed at FOB-3. The endearment "Your ass is mine" was never more meaningful.

Life on the northern sector of the FOB was spent observing day and night. CPT Clarke's bunker had an observation area on top where the observer had a sniper rifle for engaging targets of opportunity. Additionally, he used a compass and flash-to-bang time to try and pin-point NVA artillery so that counterbattery fire could be employed. (He would observe the location of the enemy fire and sight it with the compass while counting the time until he heard the sound of the round being fired. Knowing the speed of sound—about a kilometer per second—one could calculate the location of the enemy artillery.) It was truly rewarding when such fire could be employed and success was noted as shown by secondary explosions. This highlights the most frustrating part of the siege period—the NVA could shoot its artillery, rockets, and mortars all day and night and the defenders could do little but dodge. The enemy was well out of range of the average defender, invisible but deadly.

The observer on top of the bunker also had a large Night Observation Device (NOD), a large, tripod-mounted, passive night vision device that allowed the observer to watch an area out to several hundred meters at night. It was infrequent to see any enemy activity. In the few instances where a small NVA patrol was spotted, it was possible to direct small arms fire into the area using the range cards that each fighting position had prepared. Getting the Bru PFs to be disciplined in their fire and to use a range card that highlighted sectors of fire and used aiming stakes to direct fire into selected sectors was difficult, but eventually successful.

Life during this period was difficult but not impossible if one maintained good personal habits—shaving every day and brushing one's teeth became important events, as water was in short supply. C-4 explosive was burned to warm water in a canteen cup which was then added to some cold water in the helmet, which was also one's wash basin, to have enough to thoroughly soak the face and wash one's hands. Some people did not follow these simple personal hygiene tasks and had to be cajoled into taking care of themselves. This was one of the hardest tasks that the leadership had to work with.

The normal ration cycle was two meals a day. Each meal was C-rations. Those at FOB-3 were fortunate to have Vietnamese and Bru soldiers under their command as they were able to occasionally scrounge one of their rations that included rice and fish parts. By using the rice and mixing it with different C-ration meals one was able to create some interesting "stews."

An exception to this routine occurred one night when several of the officers celebrated the promotion of one of their own. They spent part of the evening in the secure FOB-3 "million dollar bunker" sipping on some scotch that was left from before the siege days. Working back to the bunker using the communications trenches was more difficult than normal that night.

Rumor control was an important task. The people on the line were denied information about what was happening—no daily *Stars and Stripes*, though we did get several week-old copies occasionally. In those cases some-one would read the news to the Vietnamese and Bru. With respect to rumors, dates in North Vietnamese history seemed to take on a life of their own. Every week or so the word came down that on such and such a date the North Vietnamese were going to celebrate such and such anniversary by making an assault. The result was everyone going on heightened alert. Nothing ever happened—a source of frustration for all.

Life in the trenches was most miserable when it rained. The trenches would become muddy and low areas, other than sleeping bunkers, had to be dug for drains. Drainage ditches had to be dug to route water around the sleeping bunkers, which were generally lower than the fighting positions. Every fighting position had a grenade sump for a grenade to be kicked into should one be thrown into the position, the idea being to limit the shrapnel from an exploding grenade by having it absorbed by the ground around the sump and directed only outwards from the hole. The problem was that the sumps were the first place to fill up with rain and mud and the last to dry out. It was amazing how fast many simple concepts of engineering and fluid dynamics were put to work in this maze of trenches and sandbags.

There were ground probes and attacks during this period, but enemy movement toward the Combat Base was generally detected early and air and artillery quickly attacked the NVA formations. The use of sensors monitoring on the ground or in the air, coupled with available firepower resources—air, artillery, and mortars—were highly effective in engaging enemy formations. The sensors became objects of great praise. COL Lounds said, "I think the casualties would have almost doubled (without the sensors)."

One of the analysts was less modest in his praise of sensor technology. Physicist Kenneth Case from University of California, San Diego, claimed that the sensors indicated when the enemy was massing for attacks against the base, allowing the deployment of aerial and artillery bombardment, which destroyed them. "That's how the Marines got out of Khe Sanh," according to Case.

The sensors were a precursor to what was done in Afghanistan using ground-based Special Forces to control the firepower. At no time was there a threat that the Combat Base would be overrun. In fact, over time the threat lessened, as some of the units investing Khe Sanh were withdrawn and later ended up fighting in Hue.

THE BRU

CPT Clarke remembers:

The biggest problem at FOB-3 was the morale of the Bru. In mid-to-late February, the Bru started becoming concerned about their families. They had watched as the entire area was bombed relentlessly. After the fall of Lang Vei and the turning away of the civilians and military that turned up at the Combat Base seeking protection, the Bru PFs became quite concerned for the safety of their families. We finally selected two individuals from each village, dressed them as natives, and sent them home. Their mission was to find out what was happening and to encourage their villages to come to the Combat Base for evacuation. Within several days 1,500 Bru showed up for evacuation.

When they showed up at the Combat Base they were denied access. They were taken into FOB-3 where we fed them and cared for them until the Marines allowed them to be back hauled on resupply CH-46 helicopters to Cam Lo. I was told that COL Lounds was so mad at me because these Bru had sought refuge from the war that I had better stay out of his way. He never did mention it to me personally. This evacuation went off fairly smoothly, though the NVA did try to shell the FOB-3 Landing Zone as the helicopters came in to load the Bru.

CPT Clarke was blown off of his feet eight times as he directed helicopters to land and had his uniform trouser leg shredded by shrapnel but received no serious wounds.

Keeping his radio relay connection to Quang Tri open throughout the siege, CPT Clarke was able to report to the Province Advisory Team that the refugees were enroute—both those that walked and those that were taken out by air. There were several helicopter evacuations. The one described above was the biggest. The appropriate resources were waiting when the Bru reached Dong Ha. The Bru were relocated to Cua Valley. SFC Perry became part of the team that went to Cua Valley and established a dispensary there.

THE EXTENDED SIEGE

The extended siege was a period of frustration because the defenders were simply waiting to strike back. From the fall of Lang Vei until the relief operations in April, Khe Sanh was invested. Over time the trenches grew closer and the threat increased, though a major ground assault never occurred. Life was unpleasant.

It almost became possible to predict when the artillery fire would begin. Each morning one could watch a small group of NVA—three or four—walk up to Hill 471 and then disappear. Several minutes later, the artillery and rocket fires would start. The NVA would alternate which tube or location would fire so as to make counterbattery efforts more difficult. The NVA also had their artillery dug into caves in ravines and on Co Roc Mountain in Laos, which made them almost impossible to bomb. Extensive efforts were devoted to trying to silence this artillery, with minimal results.

There was no need for a ground attack. The political objective of the siege was being served. The playing of the "Agony of Khe Sanh" throughout the U.S. media, coupled with the continual comparisons with Dien Bien Phu, contributed to the NVA effort to convince the American people that the war was not winnable. It was at the grand strategic level where the NVA were being successful. Khe Sanh, in fact, constituted the culminating point of the war.

On February 21, 1968, CPT Clarke wrote his parents:

This junk has now been going on for one month today. Charlie is yet to launch a major attack against Khe Sanh Combat Base. He lobs mortars, rockets and arty in every day and when the attack will come is anybody's guess. He is taking a terrible beating from the air. There have been over 400 secondary explosions since this all started. The exact extent of his losses is anyone's guess, but he must have been hurt some. The worst part of the whole thing is the waiting. Of course in the meantime the defenses are getting stronger. More wire is going in and we're about half done with a minefield which when completed will make it much more difficult for Charlie to use tanks as he did at Lang Vei. Personally, I just wish that he would attack and get it over with, so that we could start the reconstruction of the area.

Personally, I'm in good health. My ankle where I sprained it isn't even bothering me any more. The only thing is that I am getting pretty tired of C-rations, but I guess that is one of the "Rigueurs de La Guerre." The Special Forces that I am working with are really an outstanding group of individuals. I'm living with 3 Sergeants in an underground bunker, which we built. It is only 12' by 12' so it is cozy, but we have 2 inches of aluminum, 12 inches of solid wood, and 3 feet of sand bags over our heads so we're pretty darn safe from anything that Charlie can throw.

On March 7 he wrote:

Our diets consist of C-rations with a little rice thrown in every so often. You can't imagine how good a real steak with baked potato and a tossed salad is going to taste after this is all over. Also a scotch and soda will taste good. Make that about 2 dozen scotch and sodas.

And again on March 7, 1968:

There are about 6 battalions of troops waiting for the NVA to attack. Patrolling is almost non-existent. What we're doing is just waiting while he puts in rockets, mortars and artillery. For an offensive-minded person like myself, this is no way to win a war, but I'm only a Captain. One of these days I may write a book on this mess. Needless to say, I'm not very happy about the way this thing is being fought, but once I get the big picture maybe I'll understand better.

THE END OF THE SIEGE

On March 30, 1968, CPT Clarke wrote his parents:

I left Khe Sanh on 21 March and have been TDY to the 1st Cav Division ever since. I can't tell you what I've been doing, but by reading the papers you may figure it out and why I was with the 1st Cav. MG John Tolson is the CG of the 1st Air Cav and was a member of the 1st Airborne platoon at Benning with Art.
   [Art is LTC Arthur F. Gorham, Clarke's father, who was a member of the initial airborne officer trainees and became the first commander of 1-505 Parachute Infantry Regiment. He was killed when the Regiment jumped into Sicily.]
   During the relief operation I attended all of the Division's briefings and accompanied General Tolson and many of his subordinate commanders on reconnaissance missions and trips to the Combat Base.

On April 1, the 1st Cavalry Division began Operation PEGASUS to relieve the siege of the Combat Base. CPT Clarke was pulled out of the siege at Khe Sanh and joined the 1st Cav as a special advisor to the commanding general. He worked closely with the G-3 plans officer, MAJ Paul Schwartz, and accompanied the commanding general, Major General (MG) John J. Tolson, at many coordination meetings.

The operation had been preceded by a massive deception operation that was designed to make it look as if the effort would be along the DMZ. At the same time a major logistical base was being built (LZ Stud) along Highway 9 about half way between Cam Lo and Khe Sanh.

Operation PEGASUS featured a ground attack along and on both sides of Highway 9 by Marines and Engineers supported by artillery from LZ Stud. Their mission was to open and repair the highway all the way to Khe Sanh. (The highway needed to be opened because the decision had been made to evacuate the Combat Base.) The units of the 1st Cavalry leap-frogged in using their extensive helicopter fleet. They established a series of firebases that supported the next leap. Eventually the units came within fire-support range of the Combat Base.

Simultaneous with the beginning of Operation PEGASUS, the 1st Cavalry began planning its next mission—an assault to clear the Aschau Valley south of Khe Sanh and west of Hue. On April 1, 1968, as the helicopters of the "First Team" were beginning the relief of the Combat Base, MAJ Paul Schwartz began briefing MG Tolson on the division's next mission. MAJ Schwartz's concept was to pursue the North Vietnamese along Highway 9 west into Laos, turn south along the Ho Chi Minh Trail, and enter the Aschau Valley from the rear. The idea was to gain operational surprise, maintain the momentum, and not allow the NVA to escape.

MG Tolson applauded the plan's audacity but cut the Major short with words that put an end to any further discussions: "Didn't you hear the President last night? He announced a partial bombing halt of North Vietnam. In that light, what you are proposing is politically impossible!"

It now seemed that concessionary political proposals had made the invasion of Laos and the destruction of major NVA units impossible. Johnson's announcement was tantamount to admitting that we were not going to win the war. His goal was to get negotiations started and, in exchange for peace talks, he was offering the North the bombing halt. The sacrifices of the brave soldiers, sailors, airmen, and Marines at Khe Sanh were for naught. They had won the longest battle of the war and the war was lost. This was the defining point of the war! The culminating point! From here on it was obvious that the United States was going to leave Vietnam; it was only a matter of time and definition of the precise circumstances. In essence the soldiers in Vietnam had become expendable.

Pursuing the military advantage that Operation PEGASUS could have provided would have offered a chance to attain political goals and to consider whether the war was winnable, but that was not to be. It was Khe Sanh and the Tet Offensive that led Johnson to announce the bombing halt of March 31, 1968.

The relief operation was over in 2 weeks. Most of the North Vietnamese had withdrawn. There were still some ferocious battles as the rear guard defended the withdrawal of the main force. The 1st Cavalry and the ARVN Airborne operated primarily to the south and west of the Combat Base while the Marines from the Combat Base attacked northwest to clear the routes to the mountain firebases and to destroy the retreating enemy. In planning for the Marine assaults out of the Combat Base, COL Lounds expressed deep, heartfelt concern over the defense of the base. He pressed his point to such an extent that it seemed to border on paranoia. GEN Tolson, in responding to the question as to who would be responsible for the Combat Base, grabbed a grease pencil, walked to the map, and quickly drew a new boundary that relieved the 26th Marines from the responsibility of defending the base and transferred the responsibility to one of his brigades.

The attacks continued for several days until the area was generally cleared. The 1st Cavalry rapidly disengaged and redeployed to attack into the Aschau Valley. The 26th Marines conducted a change of command and the Battle of Khe Sanh was declared to be officially over.

Not long after the meeting with Tolson and the news of Johnson's halt to bombing, CPT Clarke accompanied a 1st Cavalry Division brigade commander whose unit was attacking to seize the Old French Fort where LTC Seymoe died. CPT Clarke had an opportunity to see all of the area from the air. Flying over the village he could see where he and his companions had held off the enemy. He once again relived the battle, the Bru, the men, the commitment. But the area was almost unrecognizable. There were water-filled "paddies" where there had never been any, the coffee plantation was gone, and the village was almost leveled. All of it erased from the earth. As they were pulling in closer the pilot had to dodge an artillery round coming from NVA tubes on Co Roc Mountain. He pulled up and the shell went under them and the helicopter left the area. CPT Clarke glimpsed for the last time the village where his warriors had sacrificed in vain.

CPT Nhi summarizes one of the critical messages of the book: "I was glad to learn that American soldiers who participated in the battle of Khe-Sanh village were awarded medals. They truly deserved them. On the Vietnamese side, we did not get any awards. The unofficial announcement was that we won the battles, but lost the territory; it was not good enough! My soldiers fought bravely, I followed my orders to withdraw, preserved the force to fight again, but this was not good enough."

To the Vietnamese the losing of territory, not the winning of the battles, was critical—Should we learn something from this perspective? What in fact does it mean to win?

Chapter 11

OBSERVATIONS ON A LOST WAR

A new generation of citizens and soldiers will look back on the Vietnam experience with a wide range of thoughts, opinions, and understanding. The war produced such a tremendous range of experiences that no one book or no one historian can state with finality what we did or didn't accomplish after 15 years and 55,000 lives. Nor can we with any accuracy define the lessons that the following generations should learn. However, there are some general truths that have been dramatically brought home in this narrative that it would be wise to understand.

For those with a vivid memory of the war there is consolation in knowing that the impact of that war altered and shaped politics and warfare for the next generations. But in that altering we must take the lessons and apply them to new situations, new challenges, and new policy dilemmas. To fail to do so would mean that the warriors at Khe Sanh and all of Vietnam were truly expendable.

COL Bruce B. G. Clarke (ret.)

THE NEED FOR UNITY OF COMMAND

Many of the problems and some of the emotions that the Army and CAC-OSCAR participants experienced in this battle came from the lack of unity of command in the area. Some of them are still bothered by this experience. The three principal Army elements in the area each had their own chains of command that they worked through, separate from Marine channels. This meant, or was perceived to mean, that the senior officer in the area (COL Lounds) did not have an interest in their well-being. The denied relief requests of Khe Sanh village and the Lang Vei Special Forces Camp are two examples. As a result of these different chains of command, the players were constantly working at potentially cross-purposes with each other.

Unity of Command would have meant that there was unity of effort. All of the varied types of units would have been working as part of a team with a common and shared goal. This of course did not exist. Neither the village advisory team nor Special Forces Team A-101 at Lang Vei had any sense of being part of the same effort that the Marines were involved in. If the Marine leadership at the Combat Base had the mission of protecting the political government, would they have hunkered down in the Combat Base? Unity of command and unity of focus would have produced different results. COL Lounds and the Marine leadership were interested in securing the hills and fighting the NVA. They did not see how the outposts in the village and on the border could aid in that effort. However, if the goal was to use air power, such as in Afghanistan, to destroy the NVA formations, wouldn't increased sources of information and fire control have been useful? Would not limiting the freedom of the NVA to move toward the Combat Base been useful in accomplishing the military objectives?

Additionally, the above questions suggest a disconnect between the political goal of maintaining the vitality of the South Vietnamese political structure (including the district government in Khe Sanh village) and defeating, in an attrition battle, North Vietnamese conventional forces.

A single area commander with responsibility for all of the allied combatants in the area would have made LTC Seymoe's relief/resupply mission unnecessary and would have probably saved his life. The same is true of the lives lost at Lang Vei. There would not have been a perceived utility in holding the District Headquarters or Lang Vei, if the unified commander had expressed his intent to fight a war by attrition centered on the Khe Sanh Combat Base. The village and the outpost on the border would not have had a role in such an effort. This suggests that after they had served the "bait" function that they could have been withdrawn without jeopardizing the overall goal of enticing the NVA into a battle that it wanted to have anyway.

The control of air assets is particularly noteworthy. The Marine Corps prides itself as being an air-ground team and this is a great relationship. However, there needs to be a central air battle captain to monitor and allocate all of the air assets. Had this existed, CPT Britt would not have been successful in diverting resources, but maybe the necessity of doing so would not have existed.

However, at the end of the siege, when the 1st Cavalry Division launched Operation PEGASUS, unity of command did exist.

In the future, with the current emphasis on "jointness" within the U.S. military, these problems should not occur. However, the services are still separate and the joint commander needs to be sensitive to the organizational cultures and norms that create a sense of "difference" between the units of his command.

THE TENSION BETWEEN SECRECY AND OPERATIONAL REQUIREMENTS

The above lack of unity of effort and the resulting friction was compounded by secrecy. The concern about compromising intelligence sources precluded all of the participants in the battle knowing what they needed to know. This is not a unique event in history. Ultra information was not compromised during World War II. Churchill allowed Coventry to be bombed rather than to sacrifice the information that was being gained from Ultra. Units in the Gulf War did not know what they would encounter when they crossed the Line of Departure. A company commander in my former brigade reported that he received aerial photos of the enemy's defenses from a courier as he was approaching them. He said that he had done his rehearsing and planning against something different and had to improvise.

Not knowing that there was going to be a major attack in the area was almost catastrophic for the members of the advisory team. Had they not modified their defenses slightly and increased readiness they may have been surprised and the outcome would have been quite different. Awareness of the situation would have caused more contingency planning to be done than was. The relief plan should have been rehearsed, or at least a request for the rehearsal submitted. Ammunition stocks should have been increased and additional water stocked for emergency purposes. Given a coordinated security plan there are many other actions that could have been taken without tipping off the NVA that we knew that they were coming.

Unity of effort and a reduction in secrecy would have also allowed for the enemy to be attacked earlier and the siege possibly avoided. This, of course, leads directly to the issue of strategic military objectives. If the goal on GEN Westmoreland's part was to entice the enemy into this battle, then he had to pretend to be surprised. There is some evidence to suggest that this was Westmoreland's plan. To be exact, throughout the war the United States had given the North Vietnamese the strategic initiative. The evidence suggests that Westmoreland responded to the intelligence of the enemy's intentions. The U.S. Forces, based upon superior battlefield mobility, were able to reposition forces and react much more quickly than the NVA. Thus the NVA's strategic initiative was reduced by U.S. tactical and operational mobility.

THE RELATIONSHIP OF BATTLEFIELD EVENTS
AND POLITICAL DECISIONS

The Vietnam War was a political war—not for the United States but for the North Vietnamese. They understood that the war would not be won on the battlefields of Vietnam. It would be won in the streets and living rooms of the United States. The same thing happened in France in 1954. To this end, the "Agony of Khe Sanh" served their purposes well. For 2 months the American people were confronted daily in the media by the possibility of a major battlefield defeat and the loss of the lives of yet more of their boys. This was the culminating point of the war. The battle was won on the ground, but lost in the living rooms of America.

In Chapter 5, the strategic thinking and motivation behind the North Vietnamese attacks on Khe Sanh and the Tet Offensive of January 1968 were discussed. Such thinking, where the military, political, and psychological aspects were so well blended, is valuable information gleaned from this conflict. Every strategist should understand the long-term implications of the use of each of the elements of power—economic, political, psychological, and military.

The ability of the NVA to launch a major offensive was repressed in Washington in order to maintain the perception that we were winning the war. Battlefield decisions were also highly influenced by the political situation. The announcement of the bombing halt by President Johnson on March 31, 1968, is a classic case in point. The 1st Cavalry Division was launching its relief operation the next day and had a military opportunity to shut down the Ho Chi Minh Trail and severely set back the ability of the NVA to invade the South. The planned operation could have gained tactical and strategic surprise and also seized the initiative, as the NVA would never believe that the United States would cross the Laotian border with conventional ground forces. In 1971 the United States and Vietnamese launched Operation Lam Son 719A into Laos. Khe Sanh was reopened, the Vietnamese went into Laos to buy time for Vietnamization of the war (an attempt by the United States to have the Vietnamese fight the war more on their own), and were hurt badly. If this had been done in April of 1968 would the outcome of the war have been different? One cannot say, but it does at least raise an interesting possibility.

It was the experience of this war with its political gradual escalation and deescalation and the constant interplay between the political and the military that gave birth to the doctrine of overwhelming force that was espoused by GEN Colin Powell when he was the chairman of the Joint Chiefs of Staff during the Gulf War. It had its roots in situations similar to the one described involving GEN Tolson. What Khe Sanh, in particular, and the Vietnam experience in general, should teach us is not necessarily the need for overwhelming force. Of more importance is that military objectives be a clear translation of the conditions that a politician seeks for the military to achieve at the end of the conflict. There are three critical pieces of guidance that need to be developed during the policymaking process, before hostilities begin:

- A clear statement by the political authorities of the desired situation in the posthostility and settlement phases of a dispute—what the area should "look like" following hostilities
- A clear set of political objectives that when achieved will allow the above vision to become reality, and
- A set of military objectives that will, when achieved, allow/cause the above to happen.

If President Johnson had followed this policymaking process, history would have been much different.

In the case of the constantly changing political attempts to end the war, a decision to pursue the military advantage that Operation PEGASUS might have provided offered the politicians a chance to revisit the political goals and their related military objectives. It was the result of Khe Sanh, the Tet Offensive and GEN Westmoreland's request for 206,000 additional troops that led to the bombing halt of March 31, 1968. What if President Johnson had decided differently? Johnson's decision to seek negotiations was the defining point of the war! In Calusewitzian terms—the culminating point! From this point on it would eventually become obvious that the United States was going to leave Vietnam, it was only a matter of time.

A confusing aspect of this entire set of events is the lack of political and military connectivity between Westmoreland's desire to fight a major battle around Khe Sanh and the resulting actions. Westmoreland left the defenders of Khe Sanh village and Lang Vei Special Forces Camp as bait for the NVA attack. However, when the bait was taken the reinforcing efforts were not terminated. The resulting battle was not exploited for political or military advantage and thus the battle that had been desired all along was fought and won on the battlefield and yet lost at the political/strategic level. This is said clearly in an article of the *American Intelligence Journal*: "Khe Sanh's significance lies not in its role as a military victory or defeat, but as a stepping stone for a larger Communist plan to defeat the Americans. This plan incorporated a combined political-military diplomatic strategy that targeted waning American political will."

The author of the article saw Khe Sanh as a test. He argued that:

The United States ultimately failed that test, despite a significant military victory. That failure led to the North Vietnamese decision to launch the Tet Offensive—because the United States showed it would not launch a ground attack into the North." (This actually could refer to two tests—1.

The test of the US mentioned in Chapter 5, which referred to the attacks on Con Thien and the other firebases along the DMZ and the US failure to attack north. 2. The failure to respond after the first attacks around Khe Sanh. Both of these tests led the NVA to believe that it was clear to launch the Tet Offensive.) "At the same time, Khe Sanh led to the military failure of the Tet Offensive—because it prevented the North Vietnamese from reinforcing its troops in the South."

Ironically, various US intelligence agencies collected the information proving all aspects and objectives of the North's plan. But the Americans lacked the ability to fuse their information and garner an understanding of the strategic intent Hanoi planned with its activities.... Thus, the surprise of the Tet offensive—not its achievements—shook American resolve and gave the North Vietnamese the 'decisive victory' (negotiations) that it was seeking.

THE ROOTS OF HISTORICAL REVISIONISM/WHY HISTORY IS DIFFICULT TO CHRONICLE ACCURATELY

It is easy to bend history. Anyone may write a perspective and, according to the dictates of a fickle public, their vision of history will be added to the annals that generations will quote. Until now, Advisory Team 4, MAJ Nhi and the CAC Marines that were in the District Headquarters have never told their story. The obvious differences of opinion are inevitable. The multiple views of what happened during the ill-fated combat assault on January 21, 1968, highlight how history can be inaccurately recorded. Individuals do not intentionally tilt their account of an event. Hopefully this work will correct some of the historical inaccuracies and give credit where it is due.

Recently, in reviewing the draft Marine Corps history of this era, the above became obvious. They referenced awards and decorations and after-action reports of the period as if they were gospel. Thus the official Marine Corps history is being based upon an incomplete picture. We tried to correct that then. Much of what is written here was communicated to the Marine Corps Historian.

As a tangential issue to the above, the Marine Corps history devotes an extensive effort to chronicling the casualties on both sides of the battles. In the drafts, it tended to legitimize in the mind of the reader the concept of body count as a valid measure of success on the battlefield. In a letter in the spring of 1995, I wrote to Dr. Jack Shulimson of the Marine Corps Historical Center:

.... I was struck when reading the entire text provided, by the constant references to body count—both enemy and friendly. These references became distracting and potentially send the wrong message about success criteria. One might consider eliminating the emphasis on body count by moving the numbers to a table or footnote or some other technique that would reduce the visibility of body count and the implication that a high kill-to-killed ratio is a valid measure of success.

In the final edition this occurred—*US Marines in Vietnam, 1968*. For this change the Marine Corps is to be commended.

The JCS Fact Sheet in Appendix 1 further substantiates the concept that body count was the defining criteria of success. This is, of course, a critical point. If success was not achieved in Vietnam because we did not achieve a high enough body count, then it was important. But since the U.S. military was politically constrained against certain targets at certain times that cannot be the case. We thus have come back to the criticality of the political objective and its translation into achievable military goals— goals that go way beyond body count. Body count is not a valid criterion of success. The NVA probably had a regiment or large parts of it rendered combat ineffective after the fight in the village; however, the Front achieved its political objective and set the stage for the attack on Lang Vei and the isolation of the Combat Base. The NVA was more willing to take casualties than was the United States.

CONCLUSION

Had the above thoughts been learned from history, it is likely that the Vietnam War would have been conducted differently and possibly Khe Sanh might have been avoided. Obviously, we will never know, but we need to learn from history, learn from our failures and ensure that we don't repeat them. We owe it to the next generation of brave soldiers, sailors, airmen, and Marines that will have to endure similar tests of their courage and determination.

Epilogue

THE PARTICIPANTS TODAY

The principal participants, whose experiences are quoted widely in this book, came to Khe Sanh from different experiences and were counted among the lucky—they got to go home. But Khe Sanh had a lasting impact on their lives—good and bad—and each was able to overcome the negative aspects and to be an extremely successful member of society.

Bruce Clarke served as the assistant district advisor and was the district advisor throughout the battle for the District Headquarters in Khe Sanh village and the siege of the Combat Base. For his actions during the attack on the village he received the Bronze Star Medal with "V" device. He also received an Army Commendation Medal with "V" device for valor for leading the raiding party back into the village the afternoon of January 22, 1968. He volunteered for his duty as an advisor following command of an Airborne and Mechanized Cavalry Troop in Germany (a 165-man, 50-vehicle organization).

He believed that counterinsurgency operations would be the wave of future warfare and thus wanted to be part of it. Bruce Clarke retired as a colonel after 30 years of service in the U.S. Army where he commanded at every level from platoon to a 5,000-man brigade. While on active duty he was also an army strategist and taught strategy at the Army War College. He is a 1965 graduate of West Point and taught politics and strategy in the Department of Social Sciences there. He has a Masters of Arts Degree in political science from UCLA and is a graduate of the Command and General Staff College and The National War College. He is just now telling his story and providing his experience as a strategist to suggest some of the lessons that should be learned from this experience.

James (Doc) Perry was a sergeant first class and the MACV senior medical advisor for the Huong Hoa district, Khe Sanh area. His job was to establish respectable medical care for the 800 Bru and Vietnamese families in and around Khe Sanh, to train Vietnamese field sanitation teams and to train medics (a selected few Bru and Vietnamese) who were interested in learning how to save lives.

His first tour of duty in Vietnam lasted 31 months—he had three extensions. During the 43 months that he spent in Vietnam he earned three Bronze Stars, the Legion of Merit, an Army Commendation Medal, the Joint Services Commendation Medal, and the Combat Medical Badge, among others. For his heroism during the attack on the village he was awarded the Bronze Star Medal with "V" device.

Jim earned a Bachelor of Arts degree in Public Administration from Upper Iowa University while on active duty. Prior to entering the Army he had served in the Navy and had $2^1/2$ years of medical training. He attended four Army medical services schools, one being a year in length.

Jim Perry retired from the Army as a first sergeant. During his second tour in Vietnam he worked in the 25th Infantry Division as the noncommissioned officer in charge of the Battalion Aid Station in Xuan Loc. Jim was a safety expert at New Cumberland Army Depot as a Federal Civil Servant before completely retiring in 1996. Jim Perry lived in Mechanicsburg, Pennsylvania, with his wife Audrey and was an active member of the local VFW Chapter where he regularly participated in the funerals of fellow veterans before his own death from cancer. At his death we were still awaiting word on an attempt to update his Bronze Star to the original recommended Silver Star.

John R. Roberts, (Doc), Navy Corpsman, served with the Marines and Bru of CAP OSCAR -2, Khe Sanh village 1967–1968. Following a tour on the Aircraft Carrier Kitty Hawk he was finally released from active duty and entered the Navy Reserves in Amarillo, Texas. He graduated from West Texas State University in 1971 with a Bachelors of Science in Political Science with minors in International Economics and Education. Subsequently he entered the Marine Corps Officer Candidate School at Quantico, Virginia. Upon completion he was commissioned a second lieutenant and served $5^1/2$ years at Camp Lejeune, North Carolina. Leaving active duty in 1976 as a captain he immediately reaffiliated with the Amarillo, Texas Marine Corps Reserve Unit as the detachment commander of a Marine Corps Tank Company. This was a position that he held until retiring in 1983. He presently is a financial consultant in the Amarillo, Texas, area.

The events of January 21, 1968—the attempted Black Cat rescue—had a profound effect on all the men involved, particularly the substitute door gunner on CW2 Pullen's helicopter, L/Cpl Richard T. Brittingham, USMC. Prior to joining the Marine Corps Brittingham had been an angry, rebellious high school drop-out from Daytona Beach, Florida. He joined the Marine Corps to stop the downward spiral of his life and soon found himself in Vietnam, stationed at La Vang. After volunteering for the Black Cat rescue and experiencing that pivotal moment in his history, and the history of the war, he left a changed man. He went on to finish high school and then to college and became a California State Scholar. At University of California, Santa Barbara, he received his degree in Psychology, graduating cum laude, and then worked for law enforcement in California for about 15 years as a parole officer. Wanting to further serve his community he went to Medical School, graduating in 1990 with his MD. He was inducted into Alpha Omega Alpha, a scholastic honor society for physicians. Since then he has been working as a physician in Lawton, Oklahoma, where he is also the chief of staff of Comanche County Hospital. He is a retired colonel in the U.S. Army Reserve.

MIA—STILL MISSING, BUT NOT FORGOTTEN

It is the dead who make the greatest demands on the living and the return of our war dead is no exception. The bodies of those that perish in battle hold significance far beyond their mere physical properties. These bodies represent sacrifice, honor, and a pledge fulfilled to the people and government of the United States of America. It is doubtful that the dead themselves demand a proper burial but the safe return of their remains is of paramount importance to the living. The survivors of that slain soldier need those remains to bring their grief to closure and we as a nation need to mourn our soldiers collectively and individually. Thus will soldiers risk their own lives to recover the bodies of the slain during and after battle. The U.S. military has in place a strict code of conduct concerning the retrieval of soldier dead and millions of dollars are spent every year to bring fallen soldiers back home.

But what of those that are lost in battle without a full accounting? What of those Missing in Action (MIA) that leave behind no body, no information, no hints as to their safety or death? What of those that leave behind only questions? For the families of these MIA the mourning never stops, the closure never comes. SSGT Jerry W. Elliot, a member of the Black Cat rescue mission that came to the aid of the Khe Sanh village, disappeared during that fight and his whereabouts are still, to this day, unknown.

Jerry's sister, Donna Elliot, has devoted her life and resources to finding answers to her brother's disappearance. Here, in a very small part, is her story:

While attending the first Defense Prisoner of War/Missing Personnel Office (DPMO) Regional Family Update meeting held in Memphis, 1998, I learned that a Joint Task Force—Full Accounting Team (JTF-FA) would be traveling to the Old French Fort south of Khe Sanh in order to investigate the loss incident site of Case 1000, SSGT Jerry W. Elliott.

Jerry is much more than a case number to me, he is my brother, and I don't know exactly what happened to him. He remains listed as missing-in-action (MIA) on January 21, 1968, as the result of one of the rarely mentioned, but most intense fights of the Vietnam War. His disappearance occurred when the 282nd Assault Helicopter Company "Black Cat's" were ambushed by a regiment of North Vietnamese soldiers while trying to support the Army and Marine soldiers under siege in the village of Khe Sanh, almost out of ammo, and desperately fighting for their lives.

Prior to 1998 I had no recourse in the accounting process for Jerry other than attending meetings, speaking out to the public through POWMIA and veterans organizations, the public news media, or using my journalistic abilities to write about Jerry. Writing about my brother and other vets in military publications prompted sympathy and journalist awards for stories, but it wasn't accomplishing much in regard to solving Jerry's case.

In 1996 I was awarded service-connection and back pay by the Veterans Administration after being medically discharged as a Sergeant with the Army Reserve, 343d Public Affairs Detachment. A result of the residuals of injuries I sustained to my neck and back from a rappelling accident during training with the Louisiana Army National Guard, 256th Infantry Brigade "Black Sheep," Special Reaction Team, in 1980, and subsequent re-injuries. I had always said that if I ever had enough money together at one time that I would go to Vietnam and look for Jerry myself.

After the family briefing, I determined that a trip to Khe Sanh at the same time that the JTF team would be at the incident site might be instrumental in proving to myself, once and for all time, that my only brother is dead.

I have a deep need to know, without a shadow of a doubt, that Jerry is not waiting somewhere as a tortured prisoner-of-war, held an unwilling captive in a bamboo cage or a dark hole in the ground in some remote Southeast Asian jungle camp, hoping that America hasn't forgotten him and praying to some day come home.

In May 1999, Mike Teutschman, one of Jerry's Army Pathfinder buddy's, and I traveled to South Vietnam and explored the Old French Fort after the 55th Joint Task Force—Full Accounting (JTF-FA) Team finished their investigation, but instead of answers, the trip only generated more questions.

I went back to Khe Sanh in 2000 with four Khe Sanh Marines: Paul Knight, Bob Arrotta, Glenn Prentice, and Dennis Mannion. They were returning to their old battlegrounds in the hills north of the Khe Sanh

Combat Base, particularly Hill 861. Two peacetime vets, Paul's son, Jeff Northcutt; and David Kneiss, a former student of Mannion's, completed the group.

My goal was to find the district Bru Chief in 1968, Anha Bru, to ask him if he had any news of the fate of my brother. I was able find Anha in a Montagnard hamlet near the old Khe Sanh Combat Base, but he had no information to offer and our group ended up under house arrest and questioning by Vietnamese officials for a few days in Dong Ha.

Seeking answers to still more questions led to another journey to Khe Sanh in 2003 with Danny Williams, one of the Black Cat survivors, to verify the loss location. While at the Old French Fort the Vietnamese soldiers manning a guard tower at the site, informed Williams, and the other American vets in the group, Dale Lewis, Geof Steiner, and Steve Jones, that a few months earlier the remains of an American solider had been uncovered during dirt excavation by a dozer. They explained through a translator that they had reburied the remains only a few yards from where they were discovered.

I can still recall the hesitant, collective effort to tell me the news. I was moving about, surveying the area with a video camera, when I heard Dale ask the others, "Should I tell her now?" My stomach got hard.

The first words of his sentence are captured on film, "Donna, don't get your hopes up now, but we found something ..."

At this point the camera shuts down just like I did. I stood numbly looking at a small mound of red clay dirt with grass just beginning to root, adorned with dozens of burnt incense sticks poking out of the ground. My mind would only allow me to focus on the irony how many times I had avoided that same pile of dirt in the past few days, not ponder who was under it.

When the possibility that it could be Jerry did seep in, leaving that grave and returning to America to wait for word of recovery was one of the hardest things I've ever had to do.

Never in my wildest dreams did I ever suspect that the Senior Case Analyst, Detachment 2, Hanoi, which I had called with a cell phone from the gravesite, and thought of as a friend, had not reported the find up the chain-of-command. It would take many months of battling the US Accounting Command, and with the assistance of Colonel Clarke, for the site to be excavated almost seven months later.

On April 27, 2004, I tried to remember to breathe as the Joint Personnel Accounting Command (JPAC) Recovery Element–4 Team tediously opened the grave, a small, flat, trowel of dirt at a time. It was a bittersweet moment when the olive-drab wrappings were at last laid open.

Bitter because I knew immediately from the size of the US combat boots that this was not Jerry; I had not found my brother. Sweet, because maybe, just maybe, we had helped to bring at least one American MIA home. If so, recovery would offer closure and healing for the family and the soldier's vet buddies who continue to care.

After a brief examination the anthropologist at the site stated that the remains were "probably American", and after a joint forensic review the remains were repatriated to the Central Identification Laboratory in Hawaii, where they, to my knowledge, still await identification analysis.

Expendable Warriors attempts to set the history records straight about the events in the village of Khe Sanh during the first days of the Siege of Khe Sanh through the eyewitness accounts of the soldiers who were actually there. Their combat stories are up close and personal, from the heart, but shed no light on the fate of my brother, who was last seen alive on the ground and surrounded by the enemy.

By writing *Case 1000: Keeping The Promise* I hope to achieve understanding and support of why the search for Jerry, and all of America's POW/MIA's must continue. The truth at the heart of Case 1000, and many, many other POWMIA cases, is that there is no truth ... yet.

America must remain faithful to the promise we make to every soldier in the United States military, an agreement of honor that if something happens to them while serving our great nation in a foreign country, that they will never be abandoned.

THE BRU LEAVE KHE SANH

When Lang Vei fell the Laotian and Vietnamese officers were evacuated with the Special Forces. The Bru CIDG and the Laotians were disarmed at the gates to the Combat Base and then turned away. They and many families that came with them from the Lang Vei area trekked cross-country to Cam Lo. Province relief teams that were coordinated for by CPT Clarke using his radio relay link to Quang Tri met them. As noted in mid-February two Bru were sent out and told to have their families come to the Combat Base. This occurred and about 1,500 were evacuated over several weeks on the back haul to Dong Ha. They were held in the FOB-3 compound awaiting their evacuation. The Marines were afraid that one of the refugees might detonate a grenade on board a CH-46. This never happened. Since FOB-3 was an open flat area with trench lines the refugees were kept in the trenches until the helicopters landed and then hustled aboard and off so as to limit helicopter exposure time. During these operations CPT Clarke was blown off of his feet eight times by incoming rounds, his pants were shredded and at one time he got a small piece of shrapnel that barely penetrated the area between his eyes and just hung there. A daub of mercurochrome was applied and back to the trenches. Again Province Relief officials were at Dong Ha to move the refugees to Cua Valley.

The Bru Come to Cua Valley

The Bru were established in Cua Valley as described by Jim Perry and SGT Dan Kelley. Dan went on to a life of volunteer work that probably initiated in Vietnam:

> While I was in Khe Sanh, I was a Marine assigned first to OSCAR #2 and then to OSCAR # 3. After the siege Bob Handy took me to Cam Lo to help coordinate dealing with the Bru refugees. They walked out of Khe Sanh after the siege and were housed in military tents. They later were taken by Vietnamese convoy to Cua Valley where they constructed their typical housing. I do remember having conversations with CPT Nhi in Khe Sanh and later in Cua valley. Capt. Nhi had a difficult balancing act trying to placate the Khe Sanh Vietnamese in conflicts that arose with the Bru. I perhaps was a thorn in his side, as I tended to intervene in advocacy of the Bru. The Bru refugee village in Cua valley operated independently of the Vietnamese village relocated from Khe Sanh.

Dan has worked at St. Sylvester Parish in Chicago, Illinois, as a full-time lay volunteer. He just returned from Southeast Asia where he worked as a volunteer through a religious organization and Peace Corps. His story continues:

> At the end of the "Khe Sanh Siege" I was helicoptered out of the Khe Sanh base as part of a Bru relocation team headed by a civilian, Bob Handy, who worked for USAID—United States Agency for International Development. He was a CIA (Central Intelligence Agency) operative. The Bru Montagnards were felt to be more trustworthy in battle than our Vietnamese allies and they were experienced (many had fought the Viet Minh with the French). The CIA worked closely with Special Forces who had a special interest in saving the Bru. They used the Bru for excursions into Laos where the NVA had their storage and supply routes. The Bru had inhabited areas of Vietnam and Laos before the American intervention in the war and they would travel back and forth through the border area. (This was before the Vietnamese government relocated them to "fortified villages" closer to the Vietnam village of Khe Sanh.)
>
> The Bru were directed to "walk out" of the Khe Sanh Valley into a refugee area called Cam Lo. They were housed in military tents. Over a period of several months the Bru continued to filter into the camp from outlying areas which they had fled to escape the bombings. The sanitary conditions were nonexistent. Water was scarce and food had to be trucked in. I witnessed Bru die daily from the rigors of wounds incurred from the bombings or from lack of food or from dysentery. There was a lot of

enemy activity and Bru patrols came back with wounded in action. I helped coordinate the relief efforts, among other things.

During this period I met up again with Jim Perry who belonged to a Military Advisory Command Group (MAC-V) in Khe Sanh Village before the battle for the Khe Sanh base. I still correspond with him. He was an army medic and became part of Bob Hendy's handpicked team. Jim Perry as well as other dedicated Navy and Special Forces medics were instrumental, during this period, in helping to save many of the Bru. They provided the direction for establishment of sanitary conditions for the Bru and also provided them medical treatment.

Through the intervention of Bob Handy, the Bru were relocated to Cua Valley. He set up the logistics for the transfer of rice to feed the Bru by truck to Cua Valley by Vietnamese convoys on a regular basis. That was no easy task. The Vietnamese military truck drivers insisted in getting their "cut" of the rice destined for the Bru. In Cua Valley eventually, they would be allowed to cultivate small rice paddy areas and build housing. Bob got the Seabees to build a Bru Medical Hospital. Through his efforts, arms and ammunition supplies, material for a military fort, and equipment to develop cottage industries and animal husbandry projects (sewing machines, barbering tools, raising of piglets, etc.) were collected.

Jim Perry's medical work on behalf of the Bru was exemplary. [Described by Jim below.] Through savvy and an entrepreneurial spirit, he bargained a truckload of medical supplies for the Bru Hospital. Ray Stubbe, who Michael met when we first arrived in Illinois, was also instrumental as well as many other soldiers in bringing relief supplies to the Bru. Marine units even donated money to replenish livestock (water buffalo, pigs) lost by the Bru during the Khe Sanh siege.

Initially, a Marine company provided protection to the Bru refugee village. It was only for a short period and the only back-up support from then on was a Special Forces 'A' camp down the road. The Bru were responsible for patrols in the immediate area and the Special Forces A camp did long-range operations.

The downside of the relocation to Cua Valley was that the area had been sprayed with the defoliant- Agent Orange. The area was also a hot spot for VC and NVA activity, and air bombing strikes were called in several times to provide protection to the relocated Bru refugee camp.

In retrospect, I believe that the Bru were first taken to Cam Lo and then to Cua Valley to be a buffer zone and an outpost to monitor heavy VC and NVA activity in the area. They were pawns.

It is important to note here that while the Bru were manipulated for political and strategic expediency, this does not mean that the Marines and Army Special Forces did not sympathize with the plight of the Bru. It was because of the dedication, compassion and decency of the soldiers in the area that the Bru received medical attention, food supplies, shelter and military protection. Through the help of these soldiers, the Bru were able to survive and start out anew.

During the period that the Bru were in Cua Valley, I came home for military leave and after a month returned to Cua Valley to work with the Bru. The Province Chief liaison (a civilian—his cover was being an USAID worker) was replaced by a military colonel. He did not get along with Bob Handy and Bob was transferred farther south where he was killed–blown away by a mine. He was replaced by a MAC-V advisory group, which was later pulled out. The members of the four-man team were all injured in a mortar attack. They were caught above ground playing cards in their hut one evening. (From the beginning of the Khe Sanh Siege until my return to the States for the last time, I slept much of the time underground in a bunker or underground cave.)

Jim Perry remembers that event.

Just prior to them moving me back to the MACV Advisory Team Compound in Cua in '68, the four Advisory team members that were dispatched to the Bru ville and occupied a large hooch just up from the hospital compound were hit one night, just a few days prior to Christmas '68. Probably a small VC unit or squad in the area fired a B-40 rocket, which penetrated the hooch wounding all members. We couldn't respond since we were pinned down by incoming small-arms fire. After the VC had broken contact the team members walked down to the hospital compound. I patched them up and had them medevaced. Then a few days after that Bob and Dan departed and I had to relocate to the team headquarters compound. At this time there was a totally new Advisory Team.

Captain Nhi had a headquarters in Cua for about 4–5 months in '69, then he dropped out of sight. During that period he awarded me the RVN Life Saving Medal, Honor Medal and Staff Medal.

Dan Kelley continues:

After Bob Handy left, I assumed more responsibilities. I coordinated the military as well as the refugee efforts for the Bru refugee camp.

Caring for the Bru

Jim Perry further describes his activities at Cua Valley.

They sent me to the new Bru/Vietnamese resettlement at Cua Valley. The team headquarters in Quang Tri knew what they were doing by keeping me busy hopping from place to place with orders to remain there, etc. In hindsight, they knew in advance I was to go there. I worked with Bob

Handy, a CIA operative working under the guise of a USAID representative, and Dan Kelley, a Marine SGT E-5. Together those two did some really great things for the Vietnamese and Bru in Cua Valley. There was always a new project going on. My job was providing as good medical care as I could with what I had in stock. I was operating out of a tent. I couldn't lock up anything. I hung a sign on the inside of the Bru Hospital just inside the front door, it read: "We have done so much, with so little, for so long, we can now do almost anything with nothing." I was honored with a visit at different times by two Army generals and partial staff—one a 3 star, the other 2. They both commented that they had heard about our hospital down south and wanted to make a point of dropping by. They both brought gifts for the hospital.

Dan, Bob and I lived in a tent in this little compound in the Bru ville of Cua Valley. The Bru were in the process of constructing a grass hooch for us with concrete floor. I approached Bob Handy saying we needed a more patient-oriented facility to treat these hordes of people and to keep them overnight, if necessary. I told him I would design it, find a 250-gallon wing tank for treated water and have it run to a sink in the emergency room. He did the rest by getting the Seabees and materials to our area for construction. I had the Bru construct an LZ immediately adjacent to the hospital, paint it white with this huge red cross on it, plus one on each side of the roof. We had lots of visitors dropping by. We had an out-patient area, two supply rooms, a ward with beds made by the Bru, and a pretty good emergency room. We "borrowed" a lot of goodies to keep it going.

At Cua in '68 I treated this older Bru gentleman who said he had 3 demons up his ass!!? I looked. No demons, but some nice looking internal-hemorrhoids. I gave him a small tube of ophthalmic Tetracaine to numb the anal canal and help cure the itching. I didn't have hemorrhoidal suppositories at the time. He was carefully informed through a local interpreter how to use this product. He was to use the finger method to install it. He returned about 2 days after that and told me through this interpreter, that 2 of the demons were dead, one remained and putting up a hell of a fight. I looked. Some bleeding, but not a lot. Did he use the Tetracaine as directed? No. He stuck the entire small tube up his ass and left it there for 2 days. The base end of these tubes is sharp. And he left the cap on the tube!!? He was pretty well cut up in there with bleeding lacerations. I medevaced him to Quang Tri's Vietnamese hospital for surgery.

Then there was this Bru lady who told me through an interpreter that some flies had flown up her vagina!? She had tried to remove them with a stick! I looked—a pronounced infection with a variety of yeasts and different colors for different types. She had them all. I could get the yeast, but I was more concerned that she had had this for quite sometime. If so it could wreak havoc with her cervix, womb and tubes, rendering her infertile. She was medevaced immediately.

Four hours later they brought a Bru lady on a litter covered by a blanket. I looked. She had tried to deliver her own baby with head embedded deep in her vagina. I almost cried. Another medevac to the Quang Tri hospital. It was never ending. I delivered 25 babies while in country.

They came to me one day and begged me to follow them, two Bru ladies, to this one particular hut. I had my bag of medicines with me with just about everything that you can imagine stuffed in there. I looked at this young girl lying there burning with fever and breathing hard. Remember the Bru do not eat or drink anything while ill. The ladies were preparing to sacrifice a pig and a chicken to try and bring this young lady back to health. She was totally dehydrated. She had lost the sight in one eye and could not move the arm and leg on the same side. Bacterial meningitis was my first impression. Couldn't start an IV because I couldn't find a vein and probably could not have even if I'd done a Venus cut down. Go for broke! I mixed several vials of tetracycline with sterile water and filled a 10 CC syringe 2/3 full, injecting it in a large muscle in her leg. I mixed 6 vials of procaine penicillin each vial contained 600,000 units, with sterile water, injecting it in the other leg. I did this under protests by her family. I left and returned early the following morning. There she was sitting up, though weak, sipping hot tea. I went to her every day. I put her through several exercises daily for a long while, followed daily by a handful of American candy—kids loved it! Then I stopped the candy, telling her that I had some over at the Bru Hospital—"walk over there and I'll give you some." She did! It was slow going, but still she was moving both legs and walking and could get quite a bit of use from the affected arm by this time. I almost cried. She was a little thing and those were "whooping" doses of antibiotics she received. Of course she would never regain the sight lost in the one eye.

Whenever I lost a little one I was devastated. I cried where no one could see me. I made mistakes, serious mistakes 4 or 5 times involving kids—mostly reactions to drugs.

In 1974 when Quang Tri fell many of them fled to Hue. CPT Clarke saw Sergeant Major Hom in the TV news broadcasts of this debacle. After the end of the war the Bru were again resettled into the Khe Sanh area where they are again trying to establish a reasonable life.

The Cedar Point Foundation

In 1992, some years after he had left Vietnam, Bob Donoghue went back and located the Bru Montagnard tribe's people he had worked with during the Vietnam War. He found the survivors dispersed throughout desperately poor mountain villages west of Khe Sanh toward the Laotian border.

The intervening years had not been easy ones for the Bru. The relationship between hill tribes and Vietnamese has never been easy; and after the war it was even less cordial, especially so for those who had befriended the Americans. The Bru told Bob that during the decades of their enforced isolation, since the Americans pulled out in 1975, they had not seen one Caucasian.

Not only did the simple return of a friend after two decades of absence psychologically revitalize many of the Bru, but there have since been continued small but dramatic improvements in their health and economic conditions due to modest but well-thought out and applied annual assistance from The Cedar Point Foundation, founded by Bob Donoghue, to improve the quality of life of the Bru Montagnard tribe of Vietnam by providing educational, medical, agricultural, and direct-support services.

The Politics

Donoghue has been successful by avoiding or working through politically sensitive issues. During his fourth trip to Vietnam he reported:

> While I was staying at Khe Sanh, several Vietnamese civilians told me in private that a set of US remains was located in the vicinity of Lang Vei. This allegedly took place several weeks before my arrival. They stated that the remains were turned over to US personnel and that a helicopter was seen flying out to the site. It is unknown at this time if this was one of the MIA's from A-101. The day after I heard this, I asked two government officials if they could brief me on the recovery. I was told, through my interpreter to change the subject or I would jeopardize my unescorted status in the area. Since my main mission was to help the Bru I made no further inquiries. Loi, my interpreter, stated to me that the MIA issue is so politically sensitive that civilians refuse to talk about it in public.

Cedar Point's efforts in recent years have encountered some difficulty with the Vietnamese authorities. In its work prior to 1997 in the Khe Sanh area it had seen little need to involve the government beyond the tribal and district level. Its work, however, reached a point where it became noticed at the province level (Quang Tri province). This created a "turf war" between the local (Huong Hoa–Khe Sanh) and the provincial secret police (Cong An) in Dong Ha. Ultimately, it required provincial foreign ministry intervention and many delicate negotiating sessions at the People's Committee Headquarters in Dong Ha to finally come to an understanding. These negotiations limited excursions into the bush but laid firm groundwork for future operations.

Problems the People's Committee cited involved experience with groups trying to do work in some of the provinces south of Quang Tri. Apparently out-of-date medicine had been distributed with little information on the proper application and limitations of its use. Additionally, groups that had tried to work with the minority tribes did not seek input from the tribal leaders, basically believing they knew what was best for them. Fortunately Cedar Point had secured written letters of recommendation from the local Vietnamese officials in Khe Sanh with whom it had had many previous dealings.

It also has become very obvious that there is resentment in the current government for those individuals that had been loyal to the previous South Vietnam government. The Bru also still fear much of the government. This has created many problems for Cedar Point recently and has had to be handled very delicately. Anyone going into the Khe Sanh area must be sensitive to this real world situation. It wouldn't take much to destroy a lot of work that Cedar Point has done so far.

One whole trip was spent working out all the political and administrative problems that have cropped up over the last few years. The Cedar Point representatives attended numerous meetings with government officials and worked hard to open a new dialog of understanding with the different People's Committees that control and administer the Bru tribal areas. Cedar Point is a recognized nongovernmental organization (NGO). However this has not made things so smooth. On one trip Bob Donoghue was unable to get a visa. Both the U.S. and Vietnamese Embassies were unable to resolve the problem. The Immigration Police confirmed Bob's suspicions that his name appeared on their "Blacklist." Subsequently, he was introduced to an individual with good contacts and after he confirmed that his name was on the list, he advised that it could be removed for US$600. The money was paid and the next day Bob was issued a visa extension for 1 month.

The last two visits have also included political difficulty, but the Cedar Pointers have persevered. Since those visits Bob has been denied a visa and accused of being a spy.

The Results

Cedar Point has successfully provided direct medical aid, prenatal care, and funding to build a school and hire teachers. Cedar Point's contributions instituted a pilot hybrid-seed agricultural program and developed numerous fresh water wells. It has purchased $10,000 worth of coffee tree seedlings over 3 years to expand the cash crop. These trees are growing well. This coming harvest season will be the first harvest for the Cedar Point Foundation funded trees. Cattle have been introduced into the area through the efforts of Cedar Point.

Cedar Point has also facilitated the construction of a fish-farming venture. This was already going on but on a very small scale. Cedar Point gave US$50 to be used to buy rock and cement to construct a dam across a stream. Another US$50 will be used to buy baby fish to seed the ponds. These fish will provide much needed protein to the Bru diet. In addition, in times of hardship, the fish can be sold or bartered for other needed items. In September 1995, a typhoon swept through the Khe Sanh area and most of the fishponds were destroyed or damaged by the severe stream flooding that caused breaks in the earthen dams. The ponds were drained and the fish were lost or destroyed. Funds were provided to repair and rebuild the fishponds. Bamboo stakes were used to construct overflow cuts in the dam so that in the future any flooding will not destroy the dam but be channeled out through the over flow channel. Next funds were provided to restock the ponds with fingerling fish.

As noted the Bru Montagnards do not name their children until they are between the ages of 2 and 3 years because seven out of ten would never see their third birthday. Since Cedar Point instituted the prenatal care program no babies have died. All this has been accomplished with only small personal donations.

The Cedar Point Foundation's goals include renewing teacher contracts, negotiating to build schools at additional villages, and instituting a formal village health care program. It will continue to increase the number of fresh water wells, start the eradication of intestinal worms and diarrhea (through education, purchase of footwear, and improved animal control) and implement safety training in dealing with the vast quantities of unexploded ordnance that impede farming.

Bob Donoghue made eleven trips to Huong Hoa district to provide support to the hospital, money for coffee trees, educational support, and other humanitarian support. His last report highlights the foundation's most recent efforts and the needs of the Bru:

This has been one of our most successful missions to date in spite of significant travel restrictions still in place and continued resistance to the Cedar Point Foundation's assistance to the Bru Montagnards by the Vietnamese government.

There continues to be sporadic uprisings by minorities in Vietnam due to their treatment by the government. As a result, internal security police severely restrict movement of foreign visitors to many areas that need our assistance. Our efforts continue to be a protracted battle convincing officials that the Cedar Point Foundation has no political or religious goals.

The Cedar Point Foundation's continued persistence does pay off. Government officials do remember us. Most non-governmental organizations come into an area, throw around a great deal of money for projects, and then leave never to return. Quite often these projects have no real impact on the minority people, but merely serve to line the pockets of officials, leaving behind nothing more than an empty shell of a building for some program with no funding to actually run the program. And so it sits, an empty reminder of yet another unfulfilled promise.

Bob Donghue concludes:

We continue to listen to the village elders' concerns and needs. We continue to chip away, year after year, at these problems; water wells, medical aid, education opportunities for the children and now the latest problem, repairs to homes. In an effort to stop slash and burn destruction of the tropical forest, the Vietnamese government has prohibited cutting down trees. Unfortunately, typhoons in recent years have severely damaged most Bru homes. These homes are constructed of indigenous materials, thatched roofs, log support columns and wood floors and walls. It's illegal to cut trees to repair the damage. The Bru now have to use concrete support columns and fiber or cement tile roofs. The problem is the average Bru makes only a few hundred dollars per year; barely enough to feed their family. There is simply no money (government or otherwise) to repair homes. Unfortunately, the Cedar Point Foundation does not have the resources to provide assistance to repair Bru homes. At an average cost of $1,500 USD per home the average village requires $45,000 USD to repair all the damage. There are 14 Bru villages in the Khe Sanh area.

This trip was one of the most successful even though we were not allowed into Thon Cheng. We were allowed into a new community (Lang Vay) and in front of village elders were allowed to outline our plan for present and future assistance. It was quite apparent that money speaks and that a prime reason for success was the amount of this trip's assistance. Cedar Point must continue to search out new sources of funding and in greater amounts. It is extremely important that anyone with a vested interest in helping the Bru explores his or her personal contacts and determines if there is someone who is affluent and willing to assist us. Possibly there is a silent donor out there that would provide substantial funding for each trip, which could make a difference.

Our efforts to assist these people have been an overwhelming success. What initially started as an attempt to locate lost comrades-in-arms has turned into this new mission. Though we have great expertise working in developing nations, have always found great satisfaction in helping others, and are exceptional instructors highly skilled in engineering, logistical organization and field medicine, we can't do it alone! We need your help!

Appendices

APPENDIX 1: JCS AFTER-ACTION REPORT

Fact Sheet

The following facts are in answer to the question "Why Khe Sanh?"

Friendly Strategy

GEN Westmoreland's purpose in establishing forces at Khe Sanh was to place his power astride the Route 9–Route 911–92 intersection to support interdiction of enemy logistic activity on the Ho Chi Minh trail, to impede enemy west-east movement on Route 9 and into the Ba Long valley, and to secure a key route that he might later wish to use in a major thrust into Laos. In his evaluation, GEN Westmoreland considered Khe Sanh to be of significance; strategically, tactically, and most importantly, psychologically.

Enemy Strategy

In the DMZ area, particularly at Khe Sanh, the enemy's strategy was to build up powerful forces around our fixed strong point installations, while concurrently exerting strong pressure on U.S. and Free World forces throughout the length of Vietnam, attacking the Revolutionary Development program and invading the urban areas in order to destroy the Vietnamese governmental structure. There is no certainty, from intelligence presently available, as to which of these endeavors the enemy regarded as his main strategic effort. It is quite possible that he did not actually establish a main effort, but rather was prepared to exploit any one of his thrusts which promised great success.

Strategic and Tactical Geography

1. Khe Sanh is at a strategic crossroad, standing in the way of enemy movement into the Quang Tri littoral and looking down on the north-south routes into the Laos panhandle. Khe Sanh is 30 miles from the ocean, 23 miles from the logistic base at Dong Ha, 10 miles from a fire support base at Camp Carroll, 7 miles from the fire support base at Thon Son Lam. Route 9 was physically interrupted for a space of about 7 miles but, in April 1968, was put into useful condition in a relatively brief time.
2. Khe Sanh is dominated on the north, and, to a lesser degree, on the west and south, by mountains, which rise 800 meters above the valley floor. The base area itself, excluding the outposts, is about 3 kilometers long and 1 kilometer in width. A stream runs along the north edge of the occupied area, providing adequate water, but in a relatively vulnerable location.

The following facts form a recapitulation of the combat activity at Khe Sanh from November 1, 1967, to April 1, 1968:

Resources

(a) In the immediate Khe Sanh area there were as many as 20,000 to 25,000
    North Vietnamese in some 21 battalions, plus supporting forces. This
    represents more than two divisions and about 50 percent of the NVA
    forces in I CTZ. Readily available in the overall DMZ/Laos panhandle
    area there were another 24,000. They were reasonably well-trained,
    reasonably well-motivated, and very well-armed with weapons up to
    and including 152-mm artillery, as well as some tanks, assault guns,
    122-mm and 140-mm medium-range rockets, and antiaircraft guns up
    to 57 mm. They were well supplied with ammunition and the essentials.

(b) Friendly forces in the Khe Sanh combat base itself numbered 5,700
    Marines and about 500 Vietnamese. This represented about three per-
    cent of the total friendly forces in I CTZ. They were armed with 18
    105's, 5 155's, 10 Ontos with six 106-mm recoilless rifles each, 32
    individual 106-mm recoilless rifles, 5 tanks, and 98 mortars. Within a
    radius of 10 miles of Khe Sanh there were 3,800 more Marines and 500
    Army. And, within 40 miles of Khe Sanh, there were at least 37,000
    more friendly troops. The U.S. forces were uniformly of high quality.
    The Vietnamese exhibited their trustworthiness. Logistics support was
    satisfactory throughout the battle. The garrison wanted for very little.
    Its supply levels were adequate.

(c) Fire support capabilities in the DMZ area were impressive. In addi-
    tion to the artillery, mortars, and recoilless weapons in the Khe Sanh
    base, there were 16 175-mm guns and 6 155-mm howitzers at Camp
    Carroll and at Thon Son Lam, which supported the battle. There were
    at least 45 B-52 sorties available per day. It was not uncommon, in
    a single day, to drop as much as 1,800 tons of bombs in the Khe
    Sanh area, and this figure could have been exceeded if surge require-
    ments demanded. Then there was the matter of ammunition variety and
    lethality—gun ammunition mines, delayed action influence bombs, and
    napalm—all contributed to the fire support array. And finally, the radar
    bombing capability, either ground directed or conducted with organic
    aircraft radar, extended the fire support system into night and foul
    weather.

(d) Our air transport capability, built around a comprehensive in-country
    system of C-130, C-123, Caribou, and helicopters, met the daily re-
    quirement of the Khe Sanh garrison (175 tons), and built up a reserve
    of about 20 days of supplies at combat active rates, across the board.
    The helicopter round trip to Dong Ha is about 45 miles. The fixed wing
    round trip varies between 45 miles (Dong Ha), 55 miles (Quang Tri),
    100 miles (Phu Bai), 180 miles (Danang), and, while bad weather had
    some adverse effect on aerial delivery, it did not stop it, because of the
    OCA capability at Khe Sanh.

(e) During the siege, an average of 194 short tons per day of supplies and 70 troops per day were air delivered to Khe Sanh. This represents a total of 14,356 short tons of supplies and 5,180 troops. The total resupply airlift involved an average of 15 fixed wing and 20 helicopter sorties per day. Of the fixed wing support sorties, 12 made air drops, 1 delivered by extraction, and 2 landed. The total number of helicopter sorties reached 7,870, which, in addition to cargo, carried in 17,254 passengers. No figures are available on the total number of passengers extracted from the compound; however, it is approximately the same as the number of passengers delivered since the total number of personnel in the Khe Sanh area stabilized at about 6,200.

Intensity of Conflict

(a) The Khe Sanh compound came under fire and ground attack during the week of January 18–24, 1968. Between then and April 1, 1968, the area received a total of 11,114 incoming artillery mortar, and rocket rounds. This is an average of 150 incoming rounds per day, which was the average for all of I CTZ in 1967. The peak bombardment on February 23, 1968, reached about 1,400 rounds. Understandably, it was difficult to ascertain, in all cases, the type of fire being received; however, the data in the reports show totals of 1,284 rounds of artillery, 3,184 rounds of mortars, 742 rounds of rocket, and 5,904 rounds of mixed or undetermined fire.

(b) In support of Khe Sanh, U.S. forces fired a total of 117,643 rounds of artillery; only 14,786 rounds were fired prior to January 20, 1968. Most of the total was 105-mm and 155-mm howitzer fire; however, 12,441 rounds were from 175-mm artillery pieces.

(c) In addition, B-52 forces flew 2,602 sorties and delivered 75,631 tons of ordnance. For the 74 days, this averaged 35 sorties and 1,022 tons per day. This was approximately 85 percent more sorties and 82 percent more ordnance delivered than the daily average over all of SVN and the DMZ area for the past 12 months. The bombed area extended partway into Laos; however, the majority of the sorties delivered ordnance in SYN. In fact, 533 sorties delivered ordnance within 3 kilometers of friendly ground forces in the perimeter areas around Khe Sanh.

(d) From January 7 to April 1, 1968, tactical air fire power supported the Khe Sanh forces with a total of 15, 266 attack sorties. Only 49 of these were flown prior to January 20. The daily rate of 184 sorties in support of Khe Sanh was equivalent to the daily rate furnished in support of all of the I CTZ during the past year. Records on associated air delivered ordnance for this area are not readily available.

Results

(a) U.S. forces had 204 personnel killed in action (KIA), 5 prior to January 20. They suffered 1,622 troops wounded in action (WIA) with only 22 of these prior to January 20. Of the total WIAs, 845 were serious enough for medical evacuation. The current most reasonable estimates for VC/NVA casualties in the Khe Sanh area during this period are in excess of 10,000 KIA. There were also 41 detainees and 9 NVA prisoners of war. Compared to U.S. KIAs, this is a 50 to 1 kill ratio. Since April 1, 1968, the number of additional grave sites that have been found indicate that the kill ratio will be considerably higher. The overall kill ratio in SVN prior to Khe Sanh had climbed to in the range of five to one and six to one.

(b) U.S. forces captured at least 17 weapons and, by best estimates, the USMC had two 155 mm howitzers damaged.

(c) U.S. aircraft losses in support C Khe Sanh, during the period November 1, 1967, to April 1, 1968, totaled 8 fixed wing and 13 helicopters. Of the fixed wing types, four were attack aircraft, one was an observation type, and four were transports.

Conclusions

The following conclusions are drawn by logically relating the opposing strategies at Khe Sanh with the documented action, which occurred:

(a) The purpose of Khe Sanh was to impede expansion of enemy influence.

(b) The enemy's strategic purpose was targeted not just upon U.S. forces or ARVN forces but upon the country at large, the military power in general and, most of all upon the governmental structure.

(c) Khe Sanh is strategically located and was accessible to help, not only in the form of logistics, but in the form of counterattack forces.

(d) The external fire support and counterattack capability coupled with efficient and flexible logistical support tended to reduce the overall risk of the Khe Sanh operation.

(e) There was no significant difference in the enemy's tactics between Dien Bien Phu and Khe Sanh.

(f) Though the enemy was much better equipped, trained, and supported than the Viet Minh in 1954, the U.S. and ARVN forces were much better equipped, trained, and supported than the French of that period. By comparison Khe Sanh became a Dien Bien Phu in reverse.

Significant Observations

(a) The enemy had the choice of two courses of action relative to Khe Sanh—they could have attacked or bypassed the position. A victory by them would have opened the western approaches to the northern provinces of SVN. Since the objective was a strong US/GVN position, it also would have given the enemy an extensive psychological and propaganda advantage. Accordingly, they concentrated approximately two well-organized and fully equipped divisions against half a division of friendly troops who were relatively immobile. Also, the enemy underestimated the logistic and fire power support capability of U.S. forces. This resulted in 20,000 to 25,000 NVA troops engaging in a lengthy and unsuccessful siege.

(b) The US/GVN forces holding Khe Sanh tied down approximately two divisions of NVA troops during the crucial period of Tet Offensive. These well-equipped and trained enemy forces would otherwise have been available to join the attack on the cities; and their intervention could have altered seriously and detrimentally the course of battle.

(c) The NVA forces in the vicinity of Khe Sanh suffered a severe defeat. They failed to accomplish their military, psychological, and propaganda objectives and it is estimated that they lost approximately one half of their committed fighting troops. The extent of their defeat becomes more apparent as our forces, now conducting operations in the Khe Sanh area, gather mounting evidence in the form of ammunition and equipment caches, enemy bodies in mass graves, and battered fortifications.

This report prepared by: CDR J.H. Cullen, U.S. Navy, LTC J. M. Bohen, U.S. Army, MAJ R.C. Lyons, U.S. Air Force, Combat Malysis Group J-3 (April 17, 1968).

APPENDIX 2: *WICHITA EAGLE*, APRIL 4, 1968, ARTICLE[1]

"Capt. Clarke talked of tribal heritage of Khe Sanh defenders. Beverly Deepe, news correspondent, interviewed Wichitan during battle pause." Courtesy of the *Wichita Eagle*.

Wichitan Key Man in Khe Sanh Defense

When the siege of the beleaguered combat base at Khe Sanh is lifted, Capt. Bruce Clarke can go "home."

Home to Clarke and troop of Bru tribesmen *and Vietnamese* is the village of Khe Sanh, five miles away from the combat Base.

They had been ordered to withdraw from the village and to take a position on the south side of the base shortly after they beat back a strong communist attack on the village on Jan. 21. *22 Jan we walked out.*

Clarke, the son of Mr. and Mrs. Edwin R. Clarke, 129 S. Belmont, is a West Point graduate, a professional soldier.

When Ernie Zaugg, free lance news correspondent, went to Vietnam, he found Clarke in Khe Sanh, headquarters for the district of Huong Hoa.

There Clarke was filling the role of the new breed of diplomat-soldier which the Vietnam was has produced—the advisor.

---

[1] This April 4, 1968, article about CPT Clarke and CPT Nhi was mailed to me by my parents and I corrected it and sent it back. The corrections noted at that time are in italics.

Clarke is advisor to district chief Trinh *Tinh*-A-Nhi, who also is a professional soldier, a graduate of Vietnam's West Point, Dalat Military Academy.

Unlike many Vietnamese officials, Nhi takes Clarke's advice on administration and military matters. The two are young, both are soldiers and they are equally devoted to Vietnam's freedom.

And Nhi has learned that Clarke's power is as good as his word. In recent months he has found that his adviser can summon tons of bombs from the skies as well as tons of rice to feed hungry refugees.

On JAN 21, the communist forces hit the village of Khe Sanh, aiming for the district headquarters defended by the local militia under the command of the district chief, who is always an army officer.

The communists telegraphed their attack by hurling an artillery and rocket barrage at the Khe Sanh combat base. Fifteen minutes later they attacked the village, but the militiamen under Nhi and Clarke were ready.

Clarke, Zaugg reported, called in jets, which napalmed and bombed the Viet Cong and North Vietnamese attacking force. Heavy gunships strafed and fired rockets into the area, leaving 600 enemy dead outside the village compound. The defenders lost six men *and 32 wounded.*

Two other small village posts were badly hit, however, and the military high command ordered Clarke to withdraw the village force within the defense perimeter of the combat base.

We were low on ammo, out of water, and they didn't want to commit the resources to hold the place.

THE NEXT DAY, Clarke, Nhi and his government and 160 soldiers hiked the five miles through the jungle to the base where they are now. *Almost the hairiest experience of my life. When I went back in that afternoon was the hairiest!*

Within the next two days the entire village population of 16,000 *not hardly 9000* in the village and surrounding hamlets had left the area. Half *(89%)* of the people were of the stoneage *not quite* Bru tribe which had come in from the jungle in 1962 when Viet Cong pressure increased.

Many of the Bru hiked 25 miles with their children and household goods to Cam Lo. This time Clarke called for rice, blankets and building materials to aid the refugees. Another 3,000 Bru melted back into the jungle, where they will be more or less under domination of the communists, serving their Army as carriers and cooks.

CLARKE NOW IS adviser to a district government in exile. He and Nhi and their troops, Bru and Vietnamese militia led by Army men of the US Special Forces and strengthened by Marine units, have guarded an extended thumb of the combat base against the expected assault of the enemy.

The Bru are not the most warlike of the 23 tribes of the Montagnards *true* who live in the highlands, a strategic area for Viet Cong and North Vietnamese infiltration.

Nor are the Bru in Khe Sanh all veterans of the war. Most of them are young recruits, *(3 or 4 years of paramilitary experience)* interlaced with Bru who fought on the French side in years past or on the side of the Vietminh against the French.

ALWAYS REGARDED as potential allies for anyone fighting Vietnam, the Montagnards have been manipulated, wooed and bought by whomever wished their service as soldiers and guides.

The Montagnards like Americans as much as they dislike Vietnamese, Communist or otherwise. The Army Special Forces or Green Berets are specialists in leading the tribesmen. There are about 100 forts of the Green Berets, scattered through the highlands with 12 Americans in each leading about 300 troops.

The Bru are a stolid people accustomed to the death and suffering that has lingered in Vietnam for decades. Their hearts are as hard as the jungle law under which they live. *Not quite true.*

THE DEFENDERS believe Khe Sanh may have a significant place in history. It at least should decide the fate of the Bru tribe's people and the district of Huong Hoa for some time to come. But so certain are Clarke and Nhi of victory that they have drawn up detailed plans for reconstructing the village of Khe Sanh and other district hamlets.

"We will go back," says Clarke.

LT Clarke standing in front of the Advisor's bunker with the Northwestern corner of the compound in the background. The picture shows the mustache that was cut off on Thanksgiving evening. Note the tin roof over the bunker in background as described in the text.

Corpsman Roberts

Jerry Elliot

SFC "Doc" Perry

SFC Perry following his tour in Vietnam

Advisory team: Major Whitenack, SFC King, LT Clarke, SFC Perry, SFC Humphries, SP4 Gehrke (in front)

Anha, Bru Chief; CPT Nhi, LT Phao, Nhi's Executive Officer; Sergeant Major Hom

Advisor's bunker

Housekeeper with child escaping from Khe Sanh on January 22, 1968. Courtesy of the U.S. National Archives.

APPENDIX 4: NVA PLAN

NVA Order of Battle, Huong Hoa Subsector, January 21, 1968.[2]

December 6, 1967. Central Party Military Committee established Command Headquarters and Party Committee for the Highway 9-Khe Sanh Campaign

Commander—MG Tran Quy Hai, assistant chief of staff, PAVN General Staff

Political Commissar—Comrade Le Quang Dao, deputy director of the General Political Directorate for PAVN.

Command post for the Campaign headquarters established as Sap Lit, located near 48QXD6666 (near borders of North-South Vietnam and Laos in the southwestern end of the DMZ).

Objective of the opening attacks of the campaign was for elements of the PAVN 325th Division to attack highpoint (hill 861) near 48QXD803443, and elements of the 304th Division to attack Huong Hoa Subsector (a.k.a. Khe Sanh, on Highway 9, near 48QXD857387) during the night of January 20, 1968, and draw American and Republic of Vietnam Armed Forces relief forces from Tan Lam (a.k.a. "Rockpile") and Ca Lu and attack them.

January 9, 1968. Campaign Headquarters assigned responsibility for the area south of the Khe Sanh Combat Base including the Huong Hoa subsector, to the 304th Infantry Division.

Command post for the 304th Division established near Lang Troai (near 48QXD7734—on the border of Vietnam and Laos south of Lang Vei.)

January 20–23, 1968. The 7th Battalion, 66th Regiment, 304th Division, supported by unspecified artillery units (probably drawn from the 675th or 45th Artillery Regiments) attacked and occupied Huong Hoa subsector. Its mission was to seize and hold this.

Prior to the 7th Battalion's attack on Huong Hoa Subsector the 9th Regiment, 304th Division sent one platoon to occupy the Ku Boc road junction (near 48QXD861395—the junction of the road to Combat Base and route 9), and another platoon to occupy the high ground vicinity of Hill 471 with orders to hold these two features at all costs and to place one battalion close to Highway 9, prepared to attack any relief forces that might approach Huong Hoa subsector overland along Highway 9 from Tam Lam and Ca Lu, and to counter any attempt to insert relief forces by air assault in the area south and southeast of the Ku Boc road junction.

The 7th Battalion, 66th Regiment, began moving at 1200 hours, January 20, but its route of march had just been hit by an enemy B-52 air strike and

---

[2] Memorandum for Record by Robert J. Destatte, senior analyst DPMO/RA Case 1000—Jerry Elliot dated July 23, 1999.

fallen trees were scattered all about, causing the unit to advance slowly and many elements to become lost. It was 0400 on the morning of January 21 before the majority of the unit arrived at the assembly point. Determined to hold firmly to the coordinated schedule for opening the campaign, the regimental commander issued orders to open fire at 0445.

The Huong Hoa district administrative headquarters and military sub-sector post lie directly on Highway 9, and was manned by two companies of Republic of Vietnam forces. Because this position was in the center of Khe Sanh, the enemy considered Huong Hoa subsector to be its most secure location.

At 0200 hours on the morning of the 21st, the 304th and 325th Divisions' artillery positions, the D 74 artillery units (this was the first appearance of their new 122-mm-long barrel artillery guns on the battlefield), and the High Command's 675th and 45th Rocket Artillery Regiments received orders to place intense fire on the enemy airfields, command posts and artillery positions at Ta Con (Khe Sanh Combat Base) Huong Hoa, and hills 471 and 861.

An unprecedented lashing of thunder and lightening unexpectedly poured down on the Khe Sanh area. At the same time, in the eastern sector, our artillery rained shells into the enemy's largest fire support base (Camp Carroll).

Contending with our artillerymen's fierce and prolonged barrage, the enemy failed to grasp its adversary's intentions and the 7th Battalion's forces quickly opened a breach and poured en masse into the Huong Hoa district subsector military post. Because this was an attack against a solidly fortified position during daylight hours, under circumstances in which there had been little time to prepare, the fighting became extremely difficult. The battle continued through the entire day of the 21st, and it wasn't until 0930 hours on the morning of the January 22 that our forces gained complete control of the post. The battle illustrated the determination of our cadre and soldiers to fight and to win, to accept the risk of sacrificing their lives for victory. Comrade Nguyen Van Thieng, the commander of the 7th Battalion, was killed. Nearly the entire command element of the 2nd company became casualties, the only officer left was its political officer, To Cong Kien, who suffered a broken arm, but continued to command the fighting until the battle ended.

Just as we anticipated, when we opened fire against Huong Hoa, the enemy inserted the 258th Regional Force Company by air assault into Ku Boc. The 11th Company, 9th Battalion was waiting for them there. Because the unit had carried out good deception and maintained good security, our men were able to wait until the enemy had inserted its troops and then opened fire and annihilating nearly the entire company. A number of survivors, including the company commander, 1st LT Nguyen Dinh Thiep, fled in the direction of Lang Khoai and were captured alive by soldiers of the 9th Regiment.

During this engagement, comrade squad leader Tran Dinh Ky fired one B-40 round that destroyed a helicopter and 12 enemy soldiers, after which he guided the men in his squad to destroy another helicopter.

The 66th Regiment strictly implemented the Front's orders to open fire at the scheduled time, and accomplish the division's mission with high determination. Although we did not completely annihilate it—a large number of the enemy were able to flee to Lang Vay—we did occupy Huong Hoa subsector, seized a store house of provisions that solved one the front's biggest difficulties at that time, and helped the division establish conditions for developing the attack.

These and other details of the plan are shown on the following map overlay.

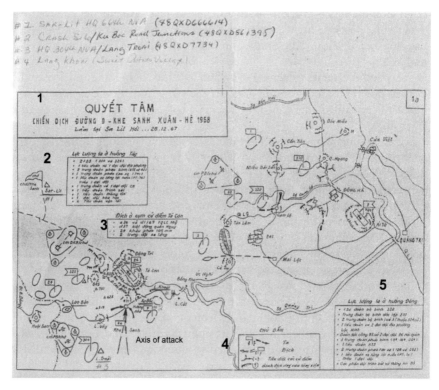

"PAVN Order of Battle, Huong Hoa Subsector, 21 January 1968 (Case 1000)" as quoted by Robert J. Destatte, Senior Analyst DPMO/RA Case 1000—Jerry Elliot dated 1999.

The above battle overlay shows the boundaries between the two divisions. It shows the locations of U.S. elements (26th Marines at KSCB and Hill 861, Camp Carroll, Cam Lo, Dong Ha, Con Thien, Quang Tri, and Lang Vei).The plan includes a main effort against the south of the District

Headquarters with supporting attacks from the west and east. The attack from the west is the attack against CAC-O2 and the attack from the east is the effort that set up mortars in the vicinity of the police station. The overlay shows the possible ambush on route 9 north of Ca Lu. Finally, the overlay tends to show the plan to invest the combat base.

The following numbers relate to the portions of the above and contain the translation;

1. Operation, military action campaign Spring–Summer 1968. Plan and sketch at Sa Lit Hoi, December 18, 1967

2. Our forces from the West Side
   - 1 Battalion and one local company
   - 2 Regiments of artillery
   - 1 Regiment
   - 1 Amphibian battalion
   - 1 Additional company
   - 1 Regiment and 1 company of CA
   - 1 Battalion of spy *(probably reconnaissance)*
   - 1 Battalion of correspondent *(probably communications)*
   - 1 Chemical company
   - 1 Transportation battalion

3. American headquarters (flag shows 26th Regiment)—a*t this point there was only 1 battalion of Marines scattered around the area*
   - Raiding party of deceitful Vietnamese *(Probably FOB-3)*
   - 24 105 guns
   - 2 Platoons of tanks

4. Note—*these are the notes that explain the graphical depiction on the overlay*
   Us
   Enemy
   Destroy the important bases
   Military camp of enemy reinforcement

5. Our Forces from the East Side
   - 1 Infantry Division
   - Regiment of independent infantry
   - 2 Regiment of infantry 1 and 3 (old S24)
   - 1 Battalion and 2 local companies in Loc Minh
   - Special corps and 2 companies of navy
   - 3 Regiments of artillery

- 1 A 72 battalion
- 2 Regiments
- 1 Amphibian battalion
- Sections of Reconnaissance

Comments: The amphibian battalion is probably the unit that contained the PT 76 tanks (amphibious tanks) that were used at Lang Vei. The overlay shows a Front and two Division Headquarters around Khe Sanh, but the troop list does not reflect that many infantry forces.

APPENDIX 5: RECENTLY UNCLASSIFIED INTELLIGENCE

The generals, knowing by November, 1967, that the NVA were about to wage a major offensive around the end of January, 1968, had assumed Camp Carroll to be the target. At a gathering of generals and intelligence staffs and technicians, the technicians from SIGINT convinced the generals that the main target would be Khe Sanh.

GEN Starbird [head of Defense Communications Planning Group (DCPG), a CIA-funded component of the Department of Defense formed to develop electronic sensors as part of the "McNamara line"] visited Hill 881-South on November 9, 1967. By this time a small detachment from the III MAF 1st Radio Company had erected a small tent near the western edge of the LZ, and inside was a lone Marine with the loop radio direction finder (RDF), yelling—but not heard above the noise of the helicopters on the LZ: "you're really not supposed to be here, Sir!" The general and CPT Bruce Greene, CO of B/1/26, walked to the northern edge of the LZ and the general pointed ominously to the north. The next day, the Marine Corps Birthday, COL Lounds addressed the 26th Marines on that hill with the even more ominous words, "You all will soon be in the American history books." On December 13, 1967, reinforcement of Khe Sanh began with the arrival of 3/26. The documents state that "Reinforcement could not progress too quickly lest the NVA be aware we knew their intentions." Accordingly, 2/26 didn't arrive until January 17.

In the meantime, knowing Khe Sanh would be hit, the first phase of Operation NIAGARA was launched on January 5. (Operation NIAGARA was to be a saturation by B-52s of the area around Khe Sanh set to commence, interestingly, on January 21, and Phase I, beginning January 5, was for target-selection.) The operation was approved by the American Ambassador to Laos (Sullivan) on January 16 and by CINCPAC on January 17. On January 10, 1968, CIA concluded Khe Sanh was to be the target of a major NVA attack. On January 12, GEN Westmoreland requested JCS declassify COFRAM munitions (Controlled Fragmentation, also known as "Firecracker") for use in nonpopulated areas of I Corps (i.e., Khe Sanh). On January 13, a portion of the ammunition dump was relocated. On January 14, III MAF was directed to review the plans for support of Lang Vei should it be attacked. On January 16, ASRAT BRAVO arrived at Khe Sanh. On January 18, GEN Westmoreland diverted electronic sensors to the Khe Sanh area (from their intended Ho Chi Minh Trail targets); they were seeded at Khe Sanh on January.

The documents recently released by NSA bring the following to light:

• A SECRET SPOKE document states: "Preparations for the Tet Offensive of 1968 got underway in some areas of South Vietnam during October 1967, about the time that the Communists were preparing for more

pointed activity in three widely separated areas of the country—Khe
Sanh, Dak To, and areas of Military Region 10.

- In a SECRET SAVIN report of January 25, 1968, NSA reported: "During the past week, SIGINT has provided evidence of a coordinated attack
to occur in the near future in several areas of South Vietnam. Many
of these messages have referred to an impending 'N-Day' (the Vietnamese equivalent of 'D-Day'). SIGINT has revealed a major buildup
of PAVN forces in the vicinity of Khe Sanh. Since October, an influx
and massing of PAVN units in the Khe Sanh-Laos border area has been
evidenced."

The following are from Daily Tactical SIGINT Summaries from the
NSA National Security Agency), All TOP SECRET TRINE:

- A developing and impending threat to Khe Sanh is reflected by the introduction of new infantry units ("terminals"), by splitting of divisions,
by "resubordination" of divisions and regiments under a new Khe Sanh
Front Headquarters to coordinate units of the 304 and 325C Divisions,
radio silence during movement, units being alerted to adhere strictly to
established communications regulations, etc.
- "The first indications of the deployment by the NVA Division was in
late Oct 67. This was evidenced by the loss in communications of the
possible Communications. Battalion on 30 Oct 67 and two terminals
of regimental echelon on 31 Oct and 10 Nov. At this time the use of
a broadcast suggested that the Division was deploying Facility Headquarters which was located 12 Dec at XD6992 maintains light communications with the following five subordinates. During Oct a split
occurred in the Division Headquarters, which in communications appeared as a new terminal simply replacing the 'old' Division Headquarters
terminal."

APPENDIX 6: INVASION OF LAOS

Letter to the Editor, *JFQ*, Published in the Spring of 1998

ON THE ROAD TO TCHEPONE

To the Editor—John Collins has done both aficionados and students of the Vietnam War a favor by discussing the operational considerations involved in blocking the Ho Chi Minh Trail in "Going to Tchepone: OPLAN El Paso" (JFQ, Autumn/Winter 97–98). But there is a sequel to his account. Westmoreland had the opportunity to go into Laos, but America lacked the political will. While preparing to conduct Operation Pegasus (the relief of Khe Sanh) in March 1968, the 1st Cavalry Division got another mission: destroy those remnants of the North Vietnamese forces in the A Shau Valley that had attacked Hue during the Tet offensive. At the time, I was a district advisor in Khe Sanh attached to the division to support planning for Operation Pegasus. On April 1, 1968 the division plans officer, Major Paul Schwartz, started to brief a much less difficult concept than OPLAN El Paso for an attack into the A Shau Valley to General John Tolson, commanding general of 1st Cavalry Division. The plan was to attack along Route 9 and to continue beyond Khe Sanh into Laos, leapfrog south along the Ho Chi Minh trail, block and destroy it, and then enter the valley from the north. Once inside Laos the division (+) would conduct a rear-guard action while attacking towards Hue. We thought that at the least strategic surprise could be attained. At the time, a major factor was the supplies that had been stockpiled at Khe Sanh to enable it to survive the siege (60+ days). We thought the division could draw down the supplies instead of hauling them down highway 9, as eventually happened. We planned to temporarily block/destroy the trail and later shift the supply base to the coast, which was possible because of an extensive use of air mobility assets to resupply. A ground line of communications would not be needed while we were in Laos. In addition, almost an entire corps was in place, including elements of the 4th and 26th Marine Regiments, 1st Cavalry Division, a South Vietnamese airborne brigade, and a special operations battalion-equivalent (from Special Operations Group Forward Operating Base 3), as well as extensive artillery, logistical, and engineer augmentation.

Tolson quickly dismissed the concept and asked if we had heard the speech that President Johnson had given the previous night in which he announced a partial bombing halt. We had not. "What you are proposing is not politically feasible," Tolson said. He then turned and left. This was a classic case of applying political constraints on operations in Vietnam. We will never know if the losses incurred during Operation Lam Son 719A (as Collins noted) may have been out of the necessity to establish political and military objectives before a conflict begins.

COL Bruce B.G. Clarke, USA (Ret.)
Topeka, Kansas

Lam Son 719[3]

"Vietnamization was intended to bolster South Vietnam while reducing American casualties, cutting expenses, and enabling the U.S. military to withdraw and began to unfold in 1969, soon after Richard Nixon became President. Soon he called for a strictly South Vietnamese incursion into Laos to test the program. ARVN I Corps, less US advisers but with U.S. tactical air, helicopter, and long-range artillery support, launched Operation Lam Son 719 on February 8, 1971 to interdict the trail and obliterate the enemy base area around Tchepone; but neither US nor ARVN forces completed the logistical preparations that PLAN El Paso prescribed.

The outcome was predictable: Lam Son 719, said one South Vietnamese general, "was a bloody field exercise for ARVN forces under the command of I Corps. Nearly 8,000 ARVN soldiers and millions of dollars worth of valuable equipment and materiel (including more than 100 U.S. helicopters) were sacrificed before the last troops withdrew on March 24. The enemy death toll was huge and ARVN raiders destroyed large stores of enemy supplies but, in the final analysis, Lam Son 719 had few if any lasting effects on infiltration down the Ho Chi Minh Trail."

---

[3] Autumn/Winter 1997–1998 edition of *JFQ* John M. Collins, "Going to Tchepone: OPLAN El Paso"

APPENDIX 7: *WICHITA EAGLE* ARTICLE—AFTER-ACTION REPORT

"Wichitan Home from Viet Says Enemy Doomed to Fail"
By Mark Edwards, Beacon Staff Writer, August 1968, *The Wichita Eagle*

"North Vietnam's defense minister, Gen. Vo Nguyen Giap, is foredoomed to failure in his plans to take over the south, thinks Bruce Clarke.

Clarke has been as close to the Viet Cong as any man would wish to get. He has been knocked from his feet by the concussion of their rounds exploding nearby at least 8 times.

Fortunately, he wasn't wounded.

Clarke, 25, son of Mr. And Mrs. Edwin R. Clarke, 129 South Belmont, is a West Point Military Academy graduate and an Army Captain. He had a first hand view of the communist push against Khe Sanh.

"You can't say the United States isn't making progress," Clarke said. "This simply is not so."

"I'm just a professional military man. I don't have any claims to political sophistication. But I believe what my eyes tell me when they're confronted with the evidence and the evidence says we're winning."

Clarke views the Tet offensive early this year of the North Vietnamese as a fiasco. He feels the terrific losses suffered by the enemy and the fact that the South Vietnamese did not rise up in revolt against the Thieu-Ky government, as the Communists had hoped, were major setbacks to Communist plans for a conventional victory.

Prior to January 21, when Communist forces hit the village of Khe Sanh, where Clarke was stationed as an adviser, he had never seen combat.

The attack was a prelude to the Communist offensive against the Marines at Khe Sanh combat base, which is two and one half miles from the village.

Clarke was military and political adviser to the District Chief of Huong Hoa district, Captain Tinh-A-Nhi.

Clarke thinks highly of Nhi, whom he described as a "very strong, very outstanding officer."

The Communists hit Khe Sanh Village the early morning of January 21, aiming for the district headquarters defended by the local Vietnamese militia and a handful of Army and Marine advisors.

Nhi and Clarke called in jets, which napalmed and bombed the Viet Cong and North Vietnamese attacking force. Huey helicopter gunships strafed and fired rockets into the area, leaving 600 estimated enemy dead outside the village compound. The defenders lost 6 men. No Americans were killed.

The military high command ordered Clarke and Nhi to withdraw the village force within the defense perimeter of the Khe Sanh combat base.

Clarke said several men exhibited bravery during the defense of Khe Sanh village and the subsequent withdrawal.

"My medic, Sgt. First Class James E. Perry, deserves to be cited for his actions. He was everywhere. He pulled the wounded out of bunkers and carried them off on his own back to be treated, totally disregarding the bullets," Clarke said.

Clarke concurs the "other war, the war being waged by American military and civilian personnel to win the hearts and minds of the Vietnamese people, suffered a major setback with the Tet offensive, however."

"It was a shame to see the pacification program go up in smoke," he said.

But Clarke believes the enemy will ultimately be defeated. He believes the enemy will be defeated. He believes the South Vietnamese people hate and fear the Communists.

"Gen. Giap is being forced into a corner. Show me a year before where the enemy left new weapons lying scarcely touched on the battlefield after a fight in the quantity that has been apparent lately."

"The North Vietnamese are undergoing something new. This is the first time that high ranking officers have been surrendering, and in some instances, defecting; officers like colonels and majors. Defections among the enemy rank-and-file are up. And how about those recent instances where numbers of enemy North Vietnamese exceeding 100 surrendered en masse."

"The Tet offensive was a set-back to Giap," Clarke said. "He has several alternatives left."

- "He can go back to unconventional warfare. If he does this, however, he will find that his North Vietnamese regular troops are untrained for such action."
- He can keep up his pressure and try to get his aims realized by compromise at the peace talks."
- Or he can increase military effort in the south and try to win the war by conventional means."

Clarke indicated during his interview he believed Gen. Giap had exhausted that last possibility with the failure of the Tet offensive.

Clarke thinks highly of the Vietnamese and the Bru Montagnards. He admitted being an admirer of their cultures and praised both peoples for courage, intelligence and honesty.

Clarke left Wichita Saturday for Ft. Benning, GA where he will attend the Army Infantry School as a student in the infantry officers' career course.

APPENDIX 8: AWARD CITATIONS

Ward Britt's Silver Star for the Air Support

"Captain Ward F. Britt distinguished himself gallantry as a Forward Air Controller near Khe Sanh, Republic of Vietnam, on 21 January 1968. On that date the Huong Hoa District Headquarters was in danger of being overrun by an estimated regimental size hostile force. Disregarding his own safety, Captain Britt conducted visual reconnaissance flights while under hostile ground fire to locate the most lucrative targets for his high speed fighters. In spite of intense hostile heavy automatic weapons fire and marginal light and weather conditions Captain Britt successfully directed five flights of fighter aircraft against the attacking hostile forces. After running out of marking rockets Captain Britt made repeated low altitude passes directly over the hostile positions to mark them with smoke grenades. The senior American advisor stated that Captain Britt's actions saved the District Headquarters from being overrun. By his gallantry in the face of an armed hostile force and his unswerving devotion to duty, Captain Britt has brought great credit upon himself and the United States Air Force."

Bruce Clarke's Bronze Star[4] for Actions in the Village

"For heroism in connection with military operations against a hostile force: Captain Clarke distinguished himself by heroic action on 21 and 22 January 1968 while Serving as District Advisor, Huong Hoa District, Republic of Vietnam. During that period, the District Headquarters was attacked by elements of the 66th North Vietnamese Army Regiment. Captain Clarke organized and led the fighting of the Advisory Team Compound throughout the vicious battle. When the intensity of the fighting increased and the Vietnamese soldiers became disorganized, Captain Clarke immediately left the safety of the command bunker to reassure, reorganize, and calm the troops. Exposing himself to the intense enemy fire, Captain Clarke adjusted the sectors of fire of the friendly forces for more effective results, and ran back and forth to resupply ammunition. When an enemy squad entrenched itself only 10 meters from the perimeter, Captain Clarke organized a reaction force and led it in an assault, destroying the enemy position. After the headquarters was ordered to evacuate its location, Captain Clarke refused evacuation by helicopter, choosing to accompany the District forces on foot. Captain Clarke's heroic actions were in keeping with the highest traditions of the United States Army and reflect great credit upon himself and the military service."

---

[4] Submitted for the Silver Star.

Bruce Clarke's Army Commendation Medal for the Raid Back to the District Headquarters

"For heroism in connection with ground operations against a hostile force in the Republic of Vietnam: Captain Clarke distinguished himself on 22 January 1968 as an advisor to a heliborne raiding force in Khe Sanh, Republic of Vietnam. Captain Clarke's profound knowledge of the entire area and exact locations of enemy weapons, communications equipment and supply caches was invaluable in accomplishing the mission of the raiding party. After briefing the raiding force of the headquarters' physical layout and the enemy situation, Captain Clarke was placed in command of one element of the raiding force. Upon being inserted into the wrong landing zone, Captain Clarke quickly assessed the situation, organized and redirected the raiding force to its objective. Under Captain Clarke's outstanding leadership, the raiding party set up an immediate defensive posture began placing satchel charges in enemy supply caches and gathering enemy weapons. Captain Clarke's actions were in keeping with the highest traditions of the military service and reflect great credit upon himself, the Special Forces and the United States Army."

Jim Perry's Bronze Star[5] for Actions in the Village

"For heroism in connection with military operations against a hostile force: Sergeant First Class Perry distinguished him-self by heroic action on 21 and 22 January 1968 while serving with Advisory Team 4, United States Military Assistance Command, Vietnam. On 21 January, the District Headquarters at Huong Hoa (Khe Sanh) was attacked by a determined North Vietnamese Army force. At the beginning of the attack, Sergeant Perry immediately converted the advisory team quarters into a makeshift dispensary. Throughout the battle, he moved about the compound carrying the wounded on his back to the dispensary. At one point, when the Regional Force company was being hit the hardest, Sergeant Perry moved to the position to treat the wounded. When one of the bunkers took a direct hit, Sergeant Perry left the protection of the advisory bunker to pull the wounded from the rubble. Sergeant Perry's bravery, initiative and devotion to duty were responsible for the saving of lives and were an inspiration to his team. Throughout the battle, he moved about the compound carrying the wounded on his back to the dispensary. At one point, when the Regional Force Company was being hit the hardest Sergeant Perry moved to the position to treat the wounded. When one of the bunkers took a direct hit, Sergeant Perry left the protection of the advisory bunker to pull the

---

[5]Submitted for the Silver Star. A request is pending with the Department of the Army to have his award upgraded posthumously to the Silver Star.

wounded from the rubble. Sergeant Perry's bravery, initiative and devotion to duty were responsible for the saving of lives and were an inspiration to his Vietnamese comrades. Sergeant First Class Perry's heroic actions were in keeping with the highest traditions of the United States Army and reflect great credit upon himself and the military service.

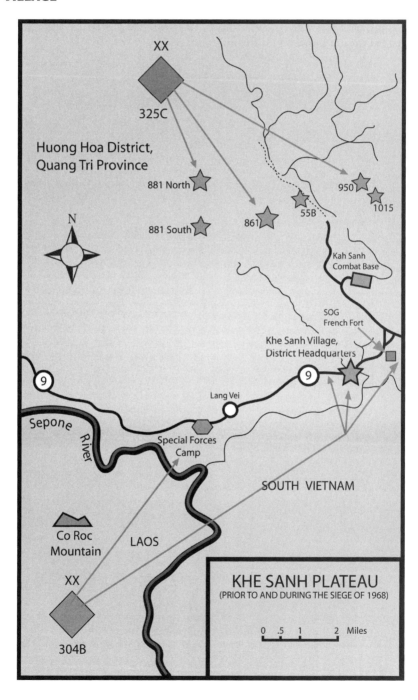

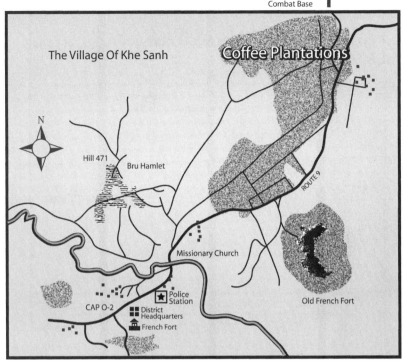

To The Khe Sanh Combat Base

The Village Of Khe Sanh

Coffee Plantations

N

Hill 471

Bru Hamlet

ROUTE 9

Missionary Church

Old French Fort

CAP O-2

Police Station

District Headquarters

French Fort

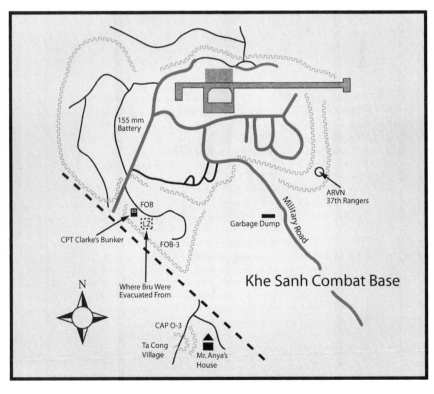

155 mm Battery

ARVN 37th Rangers

FOB

Garbage Dump

Military Road

CPT Clarke's Bunker

LZ

FOB-3

Khe Sanh Combat Base

N

Where Bru Were Evacuated From

CAP O-3

Ta Cong Village

Mr. Anya's House

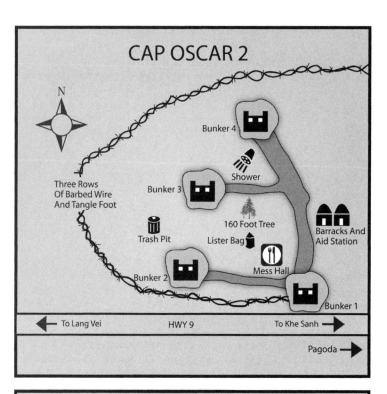

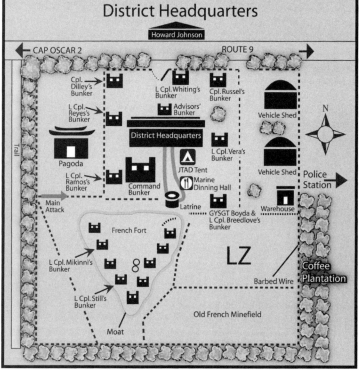

Index

Stackpole Military History Series

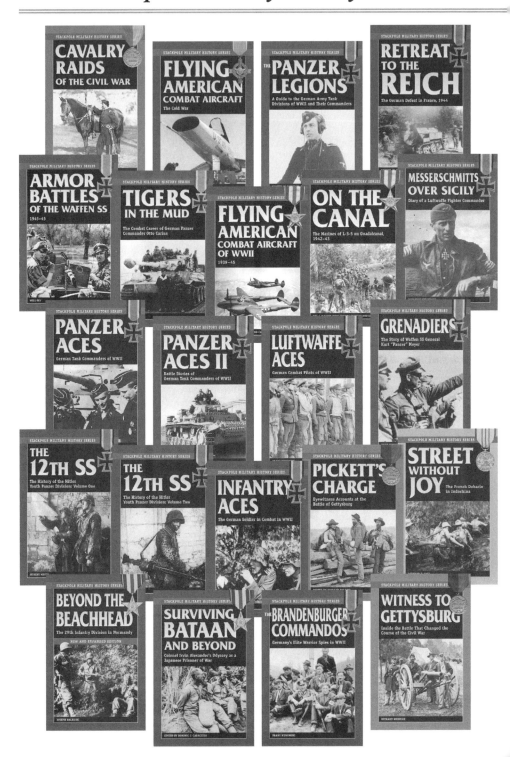

Real battles. Real soldiers. Real stories.

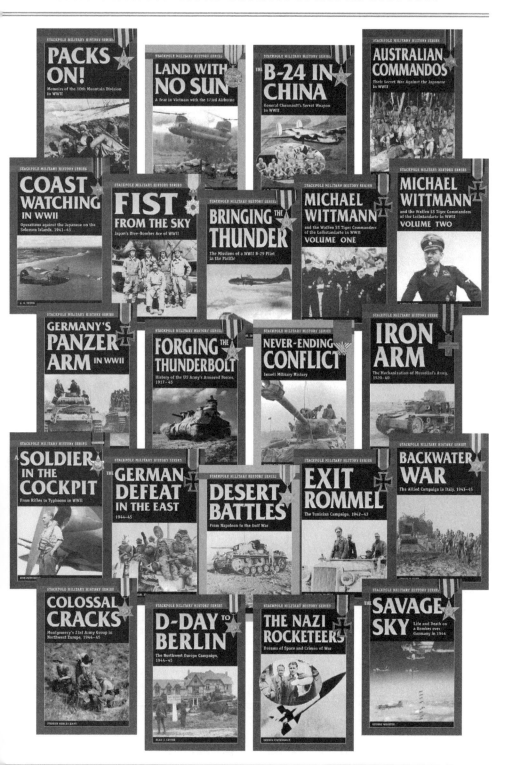

Stackpole Military History Series

Real battles. Real soldiers. Real stories.

Stackpole Military History Series

Real battles. Real soldiers. Real stories.

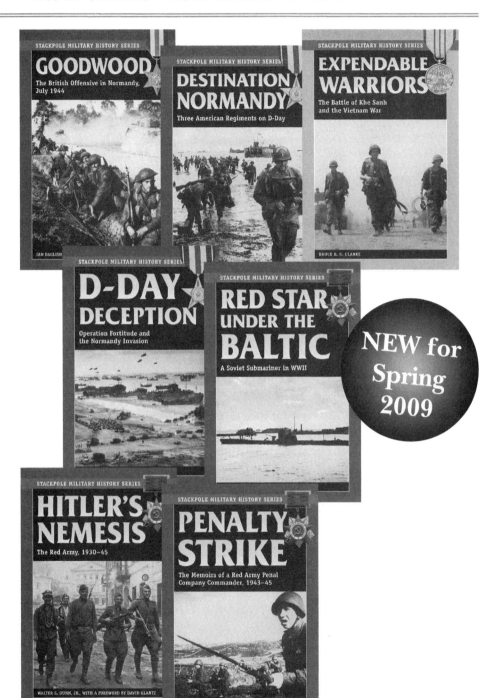

STACKPOLE MILITARY HISTORY SERIES

GOODWOOD
The British Offensive in Normandy, July 1944

IAN DAGLISH

STACKPOLE MILITARY HISTORY SERIES

DESTINATION NORMANDY
Three American Regiments on D-Day

STACKPOLE MILITARY HISTORY SERIES

EXPENDABLE WARRIORS
The Battle of Khe Sanh and the Vietnam War

BRUCE B. G. CLARKE

STACKPOLE MILITARY HISTORY SERIES

D-DAY DECEPTION
Operation Fortitude and the Normandy Invasion

STACKPOLE MILITARY HISTORY SERIES

RED STAR UNDER THE BALTIC
A Soviet Submariner in WWII

NEW for Spring 2009

STACKPOLE MILITARY HISTORY SERIES

HITLER'S NEMESIS
The Red Army, 1930–45

WALTER S. DUNN, JR., WITH A FOREWORD BY DAVID GLANTZ

STACKPOLE MILITARY HISTORY SERIES

PENALTY STRIKE
The Memoirs of a Red Army Penal Company Commander, 1943–45

ALEXANDER V. PYL'CYN

Stackpole Military History Series

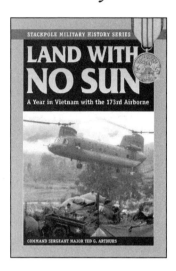

LAND WITH NO SUN
A YEAR IN VIETNAM WITH THE 173RD AIRBORNE
Command Sergeant Major Ted G. Arthurs

You know it's going to be hot when your brigade is
referred to as a fireball unit. From May 1967 through
May 1968, the Sky Soldiers of the 173rd Airborne were in
the thick of it, humping eighty-pound rucksacks through
triple-canopy jungle and chasing down the Viet Cong and
North Vietnamese in the Central Highlands of South
Vietnam. As sergeant major for a battalion of 800 men, it
was Ted Arthurs's job to see them through this jungle
hell and get them back home again.

$19.95 • Paperback • 6 x 9 • 416 pages • 60 b/w photos

WWW.STACKPOLEBOOKS.COM
1-800-732-3669

Stackpole Military History Series

STREET WITHOUT JOY
THE FRENCH DEBACLE IN INDOCHINA
Bernard B. Fall

In this classic account of the French war in Indochina,
Bernard B. Fall vividly captures the sights, sounds, and
smells of the savage eight-year conflict in the jungles
and mountains of Southeast Asia from 1946 to 1954.
The French fought well to the last but could not stave
off the Communist-led Vietnamese nationalists. Defeat
came at Dien Bien Phu in 1954, setting the stage for
American involvement and opening another tragic
chapter in Vietnam's history.

$19.95 • Paperback • 6 x 9 • 416 pages • 46 b/w photos,
7 drawings, 29 maps

Stackpole Military History Series

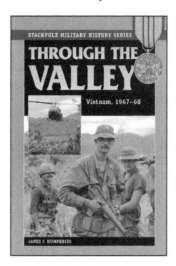

THROUGH THE VALLEY
VIETNAM, 1967–68
Col. James F. Humphries

In the remote northern provinces of South Vietnam—
a region of long-forgotten villages and steep hills—
the U.S. Americal Division and 196th Light Infantry
Brigade fought a series of battles against the North
Vietnamese and Vietcong in 1967–68: Hiep Duc, Nhi Ha,
Hill 406, and others. These pitched engagements, marked
by fierce close combat, have gone virtually unreported in
the decades since, but Col. James F. Humphries brings
them into sharp focus, chronicling the efforts of these
proud American units against a stubborn enemy and
reconstructing what it was like to fight in Vietnam.

$19.95 • Paperback • 6 x 9 • 384 pages • 47 b/w photos, 24 maps

WWW.STACKPOLEBOOKS.COM
1-800-732-3669

Stackpole Military History Series

PHANTOM REFLECTIONS
AN AMERICAN FIGHTER PILOT IN VIETNAM
Mike McCarthy

As the Vietnam War raged thousands of miles away,
Mike McCarthy completed his flight training in the
United States, eager to get into the war and afraid it
would end before he could play his part. He needn't
have worried. By 1967, McCarthy was flying his
F-4 Phantom II fighter with the U.S. Air Force's 433rd
Tactical Fighter Squadron, also known as Satan's
Angels. By the time he finished his tour, he had flown
124 missions during the intense air war over
North Vietnam and Laos and earned the
Distinguished Flying Cross.

$18.95 • Paperback • 6 x 9 • 240 pages • 45 b/w photos

WWW.STACKPOLEBOOKS.COM
1-800-732-3669

Stackpole Military History Series

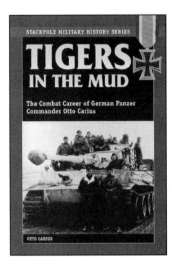

TIGERS IN THE MUD
THE COMBAT CAREER OF GERMAN PANZER COMMANDER OTTO CARIUS

Otto Carius,
translated by Robert J. Edwards

World War II began with a metallic roar as the German Blitzkrieg raced across Europe, spearheaded by the most dreadful weapon of the twentieth century: the Panzer. Tank commander Otto Carius thrusts the reader into the thick of battle, replete with the blood, smoke, mud, and gunpowder so common to the elite German fighting units.

$19.95 • Paperback • 6 x 9 • 368 pages
51 photos • 48 illustrations • 3 maps

WWW.STACKPOLEBOOKS.COM
1-800-732-3669

Stackpole Military History Series

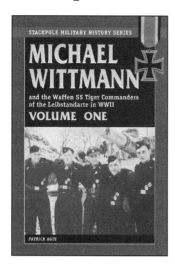
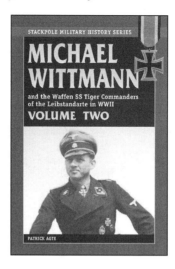

MICHAEL WITTMANN AND THE WAFFEN SS TIGER COMMANDERS OF THE LEIBSTANDARTE IN WORLD WAR II
Patrick Agte

By far the most famous tank commander on any side in World War II, German Tiger ace Michael Wittmann destroyed 138 enemy tanks and 132 anti-tank guns in a career that embodies the panzer legend: meticulous in planning, lethal in execution, and always cool under fire. Volume One covers Wittmann's armored battles against the Soviets in 1943–44 at places like Kharkov, Kursk, and the Cherkassy Pocket. Volume Two picks up with the epic campaign in Normandy, where Wittmann achieved his greatest successes before being killed in action. The Leibstandarte went on to fight at the Battle of the Bulge and in Austria and Hungary before surrendering in May 1945.

Volume One: $19.95 • Paperback • 6 x 9 • 432 pages
383 photos • 19 maps • 10 charts
Volume Two: $19.95 • Paperback • 6 x 9 • 400 pages
287 photos • 15 maps • 7 charts

WWW.STACKPOLEBOOKS.COM
1-800-732-3669

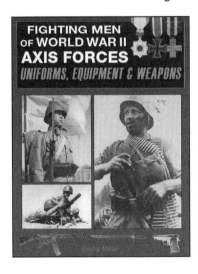
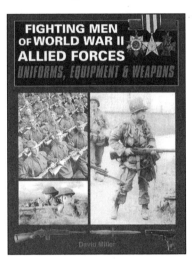